Read through the following list:

Deck of cards
Quartz crystal
Australian Aborigine
Saxophone
Zebra
Paper clip
Apple tree
Count Dracula
Pound of butter
Screwdriver
Seaside postcard (rude)
Telephone
Jumbo jet
Cycling helmet
CD player
Hot air balloon
Minnie Mouse
Paint brush
Cup of tea
Stetson hat
Tarantula spider
Football
Pair of knickers
Can of Coke
Motor car
Viking helmet
Headache tablets
Judge Dredd comic
Ship in a bottle
Cow

If you can't close your eyes and remember every item inside five minutes, you need this book!

MEMORY

HERBIE BRENNAN

Cover illustration by
David Scutt

Inside illustrations by
Philip Reeve

SCHOLASTIC

Scholastic Children's Books,
Commonwealth House, 1-19 New Oxford Street,
London WC1A 1NU, UK
a division of Scholastic Ltd
London ~ New York ~ Toronto ~ Sydney ~ Auckland

First published in the UK by Scholastic Ltd, 1997

ISBN 0 590 13479 5

Typeset by TW Typesetting, Midsomer Norton, Avon
Printed by Cox & Wyman Ltd, Reading, Berks

10 9 8 7 6 5 4 3 2 1

Contents

Introduction

Reference Point: Memory will teach you how to remember anything you want – lists, facts, names, even where you left your Walkman!

It'll teach you how to recall the stuff you need days later, weeks later, months later ... even *years* later.

It'll teach you how to study faster, more effectively, with far better results than you've ever achieved before.

Sounds like hard work, doesn't it?

But here's the good news:

If you use the methods outlined in this book, you'll do *less work* for *more results* than you've ever done before.

This book will also tell you how your mind works.

Not the whole story, because nobody knows that yet. But enough to be useful – and very, very interesting.

So read through the whole book first, for fun. Try the five-minute technique laid out in Chapter Two to prove to yourself these methods work.

But don't worry too much about the other techniques first time round. It makes more sense to come back to them and learn them as you need them.

Part One

MEMORY

Basic Memory Techniques

Chapter 1

MEMORY

The secret of your second brain

You are absolutely incredible.

You have more brain cells than there are stars in the sky. According to the experts, your creative capacity may well be infinite.

You have an astounding memory. Almost as soon as you were born, you started recording everything you experienced: snatches of conversation ... scents ... scenes ... tastes...

Every word you've heard spoken, every book you've ever read, every moment of every movie you ever watched, every bar of music played within earshot is laid down for ever in your memory.

If you live to be ninety-nine, those memories will still be there. This was discovered in a peculiar way. It's horrible, but fascinating.

Brain pain drain

Your brain is the only organ in your body that can't feel pain. Because of this, brain surgery can be carried out without a general anaesthetic. They give you something like a dentist's injection to numb the scalp and skull, then drill through. But if the drill slipped and started to gouge into your brain, you wouldn't feel a thing.

The lack of pain receptors is a real bonus for brain surgeons. Instead of having a patient who just lies there like a sack of meat, they have somebody who can tell them what's happening as they probe a little here and snip a little there.

Back in 1935, a neurosurgeon (they're the ones who get to hack up brains) named Wilder Penfield started some experimental work at McGill University in Montreal, Canada. A patient lay in the operating theatre with the top of her skull off while Dr Penfield inserted slim electrodes into her brain. The idea was to trigger a small electric current through each electrode in turn, thus stimulating the area of the brain in which it was buried. That way, you could learn which parts of the brain did what.

When everything was in place, he sent in the first little jolt of electricity and asked the patient what was happening. She told him her ear felt funny. Another little jolt and her foot twitched. And so on.

But then something really weird happened. He sent in a jolt and the patient reported she was back in childhood, hearing her mother call her to come into the kitchen. This had happened *thirty years* before, but every detail was still there – the wind in her hair, the expression on her mother's face, each word spoken ... everything. It had all been stored perfectly in the woman's memory.

Dr Penfield continued his experiments, with the occasional tea break, up to 1960 and showed again and again, with patient after patient, that you could bring up memories so vivid people actually thought they were *reliving* bits of their past. He checked their stories where he was able to and found they stood up. What the patient remembered after those little jolts was what had really happened to them, sometimes many years ago. It seems that all of us come equipped with the perfect photographic memory. We literally store every detail of everything we see, hear, touch, taste and smell. So, you with the perfect photographic memory, how come you forget things?

Two dopey old theories

Earlier this century, they came up with two main theories. The first was that memory traces simply fade with time. This sounds sensible and likely since most things seem to fade with time. The original of Van Gogh's *Sunflowers* is

13

nearly black now. Those lovely, muted, sandy colours you find in Egyptian tombs were once garish and bright.

Sensible or not, experiments finally showed this theory to be just plain wrong. Memory traces don't fade. Penfield and others have shown clearly that they last for ever. Psychologists promptly jumped bandwagons to the second main theory, known as the interference theory of forgetting. The idea behind this was that old memories are somehow crowded out by new ones – the very thing we've been talking about.

It turns out this second theory was just plain wrong as well. You can see why if you take a minute to think about it. If new memories push out old ones, then the more you learn, the more you're going to forget. Put like that, it begins to sound pretty silly.

There are actually a number of reasons why you forget, but one of the most important is that you were never taught how to use your memory properly. It was like getting a really complicated new computer without the manual.

There is a very good reason why you've never been taught to use your memory properly. For centuries, the educational system has been based on the idea that you have only one brain. This idea is wrong.

Let's get back to the operating theatre. This time the patient has temporal lobe epilepsy. Epilepsy is a condition triggered by a malfunction in the brain's electrical system. It's like a tiny thunder storm. Typically, the storm starts in one location and spreads. When it spreads far enough, the patient has a fit.

Obviously, if you can stop the storm spreading, you stop the fit. For all practical purposes, you've cured the epilepsy. But how do you stop the storm spreading?

Your second brain

Since the days of Ancient Egypt, it's been known that the

14

human brain is made up of two halves, each looking remarkably like a giant walnut. Joining the two halves is a network of about three hundred million nerve fibres. This network is called the *corpus callosum* and for a long time people couldn't see that it did very much.

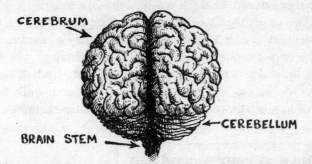

If, for example, you cut through the corpus callosum of a cat or a monkey, you don't kill it or send it mad. In fact, it continues to behave much as it always did. Encouraged by this discovery, surgeons reckoned that if they cut through the *corpus callosum* of an epileptic patient, it would stop the storm spreading from one half of the brain to the other.

They tried it and it worked. The fits stopped (or at least weren't nearly so bad) and the patients continued to behave more or less normally, exactly like the cats and the monkeys. For a while, this sort of surgery became quite fashionable.

But then in 1950, a couple of scientists called Roger W. Sperry and Michael Gazzaniga discovered something very peculiar while studying patients who'd had the operation.

They found these patients couldn't read with their left eyes. They could *see* with their left eyes all right, but couldn't read with them. They could, however, read quite normally with their right eyes.

They also found that if a patient bumped into something with his left side, he didn't notice. The right side was fine.

15

It got more weird. If they covered each of the patient's eyes in turn and showed him a square and a circle, he'd tell you he'd just seen a square, without mentioning the circle. But if you then asked him to *draw* what he'd seen with his left hand, he'd draw the circle. And if you asked him what he'd just drawn, he'd tell you he'd drawn a square.

The experiments went on for a long time because the scientists couldn't quite believe what they'd discovered. The only thing that made sense of their findings was that the brain doesn't consist of two halves at all. Each of those 'halves' had to be a brain in its own right and, while they looked much the same, they actually did different things.

You and your second self

The person you think of as *you* lives in the left side of your brain, the side that deals with language and logic. But you have another self you're not normally aware of, a creative and artistic self. It lives in the right side of the brain which is concerned with patterns and insights. As long as your *corpus callosum* stays in one piece, there is communication – and co-operation – between them.

All this explains why the way you're taught to remember has its drawbacks. Educational emphasis has long been on verbal skills (speaking, reading, writing), logical thought and mathematical deduction. Which is fine so far as it goes, but leaves your right brain starved.

More to the point, it's a really bad way of teaching you how to use your mega memory. But you can change all that, starting right now.

Chapter 2

MEMORY

Five minutes to a mega Memory

In five minutes you can learn how to memorize a list of 30 items so effectively that you can not only read it back from memory, but also read it backwards!

Using a simple, easy, right-brain technique, you can burn the items on that list so deeply into your memory that you'll *still* be able to recall them days, even weeks later.

Of course it sounds impossible, but you can do it.

Here's the list:

Deck of cards
Quartz crystal
Australian Aborigine
Saxophone
Zebra
Paper clip
Apple tree
Count Dracula
Pound of butter
Seaside postcard (rude)
Telephone
Jumbo jet
Cycling helmet
CD player
Hot air balloon
Minnie Mouse
Paint brush
Cup of tea
Stetson hat
Screwdriver
Tarantula spider
Football
Pair of knickers
Can of Coke
Sports car

Viking helmet
Headache tablets
Judge Dredd comic
Ship in a bottle
Cow

Goes on for ever, doesn't it?

You'll have noticed one thing about that list already. There is absolutely no connection between the various items in it. This is deliberate. Understand, you could be looking at a list of *anything*. It could be a shopping list, if it wasn't for Count Dracula (and possibly the Aborigine). Or it could be a list of machine parts, or a list of things you have to take to school. And if you learn to memorize thirty random items like the ones listed here, you can surely memorize any list anybody is ever going to hand you.

Test your memory here

But first, let's test your memory as it is now. This will give you something to compare your new skills with – and to prove to you, absolutely, that right brain techniques really do improve your memory. So let's see how you get on learning the list the old way.

Most people are taught that the way to learn something is to repeat it. Over and over. You fight back the boredom, grit your teeth and repeat it. You repeat it until your brain goes into meltdown, then you repeat it some more. The theory is that if you repeat it often enough it sticks. Sometimes it does.

Sit down now and memorize the list of thirty items any way you've been taught. It will take you less than five minutes to memorize the list the new way set out in this

19

book. But to be fair, take *double* that time to try any other way you know. So take ten minutes and learn the list.

When the ten minutes are up, go off and play a game for half an hour. Or eat a pizza. Do anything you'll enjoy. Rest your mind. Then, after half an hour, come back and test yourself, writing down as many of the items as you can remember. Make a note of how many you managed.

Do all that now, before you read on.

The new way to remember

However awful your memory just proved to be, you can improve it dramatically by using a *different way* to memorize that list. The new way is going to be a lot easier than the old, a lot more fun than the old and the interesting thing about this new way is that it isn't all that new. It dates back to the days of the Greek poet Simonides, who lived more than 2,500 years ago.

Simonides spent much of his time writing victory odes, dirges, elegies and making witty comments. One of them was 'Painting is silent poetry, and poetry painting that speaks,' which is the sort of profoundly memorable thing old Greek poets tended to say.

Simonides was very popular with the aristocracy of his time and on one occasion he was invited to attend a victory banquet. It was a very large and boisterous affair, two facts which contributed to the collapse of the floor in the banqueting hall. Fortunately Simonides was called away just before this happened. He returned to a scene of horror. Not only were hundreds of the guests *killed, but their bodies were so mangled and mutilated that they were completely unrecognizable. Simonides was asked to help identify who was who. It looked almost impossible ... until Simonides suddenly realized he could do the job by remembering where each guest had been sitting.*

Never one to waste an interesting experience (however gruesome) Simonides began to wonder if he could turn his discovery into a memory system. It occurred to him that if he could visualize a place in detail, he should be able to imagine items set about that place which should make them easier to remember, exactly like the names of the mutilated corpses. For convenience, he would often visualize a series of places around his house. He would imagine the items on his list as being stored in the various specific places, such as in a particular cupboard on a particular table, so that when he needed to remember them, he would simply visit the places in his imagination and 'see' what had been stored there.

It sounds a bit daft, but he tried it and it worked. It worked so well that many of his fellow Greeks started to use the system. It was later taken up by the Romans, who used it to remember various points in making a speech. That's why, to this day, you still hear speakers using the phrases 'in the first place' and 'in the second place'.

Much of the wisdom of the ancient world died out during the Dark Ages, but one peculiar group of people made sure Simonides's remarkable discovery continued to be used. However while they used it themselves, they kept it a secret. The reason for this was that they were afraid of the Inquisition.

21

The Inquisition was set up by Pope Gregory IX in 1231. (You'll soon be able to remember stuff like this very easily.) The original idea was to prosecute people who disagreed with the Catholic faith, but that was quickly extended to include anybody who practised magic, or misbehaved in various other ways. It was a popular change. Many witches and magicians were burned.

In Medieval times, magicians went in for lengthy rituals. They believed that if you got a word out of place, something terrible would happen, so a good memory was very important to them. They grabbed hold of Simonides's system and taught it as one of the black arts, the Secret Art of Memory.

The imaginary place they used in their system was called a *locus* – or *loci* if they had more than one. The term is just the Latin word for 'place'. During the Renaissance, a period of blossoming knowledge, the Secret Art of Memory finally became a bit less secret, and people discovered how these imaginary places were made. The magicians based them on large public buildings. They did this because they had a lot to remember. You've only got thirty items to remember, so you can make do with a smaller locus.

Improve your memory here

Imagine your own home. That's to say, make a picture in your mind. Visualize your home the way you might do if you were daydreaming. For the next few minutes, your home is going to be your locus, the place where you put things you want to remember, just like old Simonides.

Imagine yourself standing outside your own front door. Try to visualize it as vividly as possible, noting the colour of the paint, the shine on the brass knocker and so on. Let's suppose you go through a glass conservatory to get to the front door. Place the *deck of cards* here. There's only one problem. The conservatory is a jungle of potted plants, so you might not notice a little pack of cards. So solve that problem by imagining them as *huge,* so big you have to climb over them to get to the front door.

Having climbed over the *deck of cards* and opened the front door, you step into your front hall. Here you place the *quartz crystal*. But there's a problem here as well. The table in the hall is usually chock-a-block with all sorts of little ornaments. To make sure you remember the one you want to remember, put it in the middle of the floor and make it huge as well.

There are three doors leading out of the hallway: one right, one left, one straight ahead. Turn right and walk through that door into your living room. The *Australian Aborigine* is already there, sitting in your favourite chair and playing his didgeridoo. 'G'day, mate,' he says.

You're about to move on to place the next object when a thought occurs to you. You take away the didgeridoo and give the Aborigine a *saxophone* to play instead. He looks a bit bewildered, but that way you've placed two of your objects instead of one.

Leading from the living room is a door to the kitchen, where you place the *zebra* standing precariously on the kitchen table. One of three doors out of the kitchen leads to a walk-in larder where you leave the *paper clip*. Once again, since a paper clip is a little thing that might easily get lost, turn it into a huge six-foot-tall paper clip which you prop against the door so it will fall down with a clang the minute somebody opens it.

Getting the hang of it? Change the examples above so they fit your real house. Then, as you move through your home locus, just imagine the various items on your list in the different places you pass through.

Don't waste a lot of time on any one item. You don't have to repeat things, or concentrate, or make it difficult for yourself. Just visualize as clearly as you can, put the item in place, then imagine yourself going on to the next room, corridor, or whatever.

The method you're learning here can be used to memorize any list. Want to remember every actor who appeared in a particular movie? Paste the name of the movie on the door of your locus, then place the actors in the various rooms inside.

Problems

There are a few possible problems. The first is fairly obvious. You have a list of thirty items, but unless you're living in a palace, your home's not likely to have thirty rooms. But, as you've seen from the example, you can put more than one item in the same room.

For really long lists, where you need to put lots of items into each room, you'll need a sub-system. What this means is that you can decide always to walk around each room *clockwise* when you come into it. That way you can leave a different item at 1 o'clock, 2 o'clock, 3 o'clock all the way round the room. This gives you places for a dozen items per room – more than you're likely to need for the average list.

Another problem is size. You've already seen what to do when the item is small. You simply imagine it larger. It's generally a good idea to exaggerate the size of anything you're storing in a locus. If the item is already big, like our jumbo jet, stuff it in as best you can, all the better if it's all squashed up.

A third problem is boredom. Once you get bored, your concentration goes. Before you know it, you won't even be bothered to use a marvellous memory system like this one and you'll forget stuff just as quickly as you did before. So how do you tackle the problem of boredom?

The answer is to make your mental picture *dramatic,* make it *ludicrous,* make it *amusing* or make it just plain *silly.* Give it movement, sound, action. Turn yourself into the producer of your own inner movie, like when we put the zebra on the kitchen table. (Rather than just having it standing in the middle of the floor.) Even better, you could have him doing a tap dance or a hand stand.

Seeing is believing

Try to see the specific item in the most appropriate (but still ludicrous) way. For example, when you come to placing the seaside postcard (rude), try to visualize what it really looks like.

So, go all the way through your home and all the way through your list until you have placed all thirty items, finishing with the cow.

Now comes the moment of truth. Put the list away, take a pen and paper, imagine yourself at the front door of your house and write down 'deck of cards', since that's what's waiting for you first.

Now, take the same route through your home as you did when you were placing the items and write down their names as you find them in the rooms you visit.

Don't worry if you draw an occasional blank. This is the first time you've tried the technique and nobody expects perfection. Just keep going to the next room and write down what you find there. When you've finished, check your score.

You may have all thirty items correct (and in the correct order as well) but even if you haven't, you'll have done better – far better – using this technique than you did trying to learn the items off by heart the old way. You'll have found it easier, and a whole lot more fun.

Of course, there was a bit of cheating. The first time you didn't try to remember your list until you'd gone off and amused yourself for half an hour. This time you started to write it down straight away. But let's find out how well you *really* remember that list. Forget half an hour. *Tomorrow* sometime, or the *day after*, visualize yourself walking through your home and write down the various items you have placed there, starting with the deck of cards and ending with the cow. You will *still* remember all or most of them.

That's some going for a beginner.

Chapter 3

MEMORY

The man who could never forget anything, ever

How far can you take your amazing memory?

Harry Lorayne makes a living demonstrating his. When he isn't touring with his stage show or appearing on television, he gets a lot of invitations to talk about memory to various clubs and organizations.

In America, where Harry lives, some clubs can be huge, especially in the cities. You get membership lists of a thousand, fifteen hundred or more names. Before the meeting starts, Harry stands at the door along with the President and is introduced to every member coming in. So there are days when he gets introduced to upwards of one thousand five hundred people – one thousand five hundred brand new names and faces.

When everybody is in their places, they have lunch, or their meeting, or whatever they're doing. After this, anything up to an hour and a half later, Harry stands up and talks for twenty minutes on the subject of memory. When he's finished, he asks for questions ... and makes a promise. If he can't greet the questioner by name, he will pay him $1,000.

In all the years he has been making that promise, Harry Lorayne has never had to pay out a cent.

That's pretty impressive – especially since most of us manage to forget a name five minutes after we've been introduced – but it's nothing compared with some of the *really* amazing memory feats you come across.

Memory marvels

The Talmud is a vast compendium of law and lore that forms the basis of Jewish religious life. For centuries it's been the principal subject of Jewish study. In its modern published form, it runs somewhere between 18 and 22 volumes, depending on the edition. That's equivalent in size to a whole set of encyclopaedias.

There are rabbis in Poland who can recite the entire Talmud from memory. Every word of it. Without a mistake.

Mega memory isn't confined to learned rabbis. There are Moslems who can recite the whole of the Koran, a text which contains 114 chapters known as *suras*. In 1967, the Turk Mehmed Ali Halici showed what could be done by recording 6,500 of its verses entirely from memory. He made no mistakes whatsoever, despite the fact that the session took six hours.

In Hindu India, the Rig Veda is the oldest of the Holy Books. It contains a total of 10,550 verses, some 153,826 words, and is only one of four Vedas of somewhat similar length. The Vedas are so revered that Hindus worry about the possibility that they might be destroyed. So specially-trained Brahmin students memorize the lot.

Back in 1976, the black American writer Alex Haley published a book called *Roots: The Saga of an American Family*, which became a Pulitzer prize-winning international best seller. It was the story of Haley's own family traced back through the slave times to its origins in West Africa. Haley researched seven generations in America, then travelled to Africa to try to complete the work. Family stories told how a young, black African named Kunta Kinte had gone off looking for materials to make a drum but he was captured by slavers, and was later to found the Haley family in America. Alex Haley wanted to find out if he had really existed.

But how do you get proof of that sort in rural West Africa? Haley soon found out. He located the relevant tribe and questioned the chief. When the chief heard what Haley wanted, he did something that was nothing short of miraculous. He began to recite the entire tribal history, generation by generation, backwards and from memory.

Haley listened enthralled as the unfolding story stretched for hours, then days. On and on went the old chief, describing detail after detail, adventure after adventure, name after name. Haley was dozing in the afternoon sun when a phrase in the chief's saga jerked him awake: 'Then Kunta Kinte went off into the jungle to find materials to make himself a drum...'

Memory has been a standard way to record tribal history in many cultures. When Kunta Kinte turned up in the memory annals of the West African tribe, Alex Haley cut the recitation short. But how far could the old chief have gone on? We do know that in New Zealand, the Maori Chief Kaumatara astonished a reporter by reciting a *thousand-year* history of his tribe from memory. The story, which spanned forty-five generations, took three days.

Number wizards

Of course, when something interests you – like the history of your tribe – it's easier to memorize than some boring, meaningless abstraction. That's why you may find it easier to pick up the words of pop tunes than a list of numbers. But the numbers bit can still be done (and before the end of this book, you'll be doing it). Take π, the value *pi,* for example.

Pi is the ratio between the circumference of a circle and its diameter. Since this ratio is the same for all circles, it's a very handy value to know. As a fraction it is close enough to $^{22}/_7$. But try turning it into a decimal and it goes on for ever. Most people call it 3.1416 and if that's not good enough, they grab the nearest computer.

Except there are people who don't like computers. One of these was Professor A.C. Aitken of Edinburgh University. It sounds daft, but he memorized *pi* to the first *thousand* decimal places. You'd imagine that was one record nobody would want to beat, but since Professor Aitken's death, the Japanese Hideaki Tomoyori has committed the first *ten thousand* decimal places to memory.

Feats like these don't necessarily require years of study and effort. The Yogi Shaa, who lived in Bombay, India, could memorize any poem, up to a thousand phrases, in any language (whether he understood it or not) after listening to it only once.

Wisdom of Solomon

Shaa's remarkable recall seems to have been the result of his yoga training. Solomon Veniaminovich Shereshevskii was born with his.

When he was examined, over a period of thirty years, by the distinguished Russian psychologist Professor A.R. Luria, Solomon proved himself incapable of ever forgetting anything, however unimportant.

The results of his tests with Luria read like the wildest fantasy. Solomon, a journalist, was first sent to the good professor when his editor noticed he never took notes, but could still recite back everything he heard word perfect. Luria very quickly discovered the standard memory tests were useless for Solomon – he found them far too easy.

So Luria began drawing up enormous lists of nonsense syllables. Solomon played them back from memory after a single reading. Luria then decided to confuse him by making the syllables very similar: ma, va, na, sa and so on. Solomon recalled them perfectly ... and proved he could still recall them perfectly eight years later. Not only that, but he was able to remember the clothes Luria was wearing, the furnishings in the room and the weather outside on the day of the original test.

Dolphins never forget

Good memory isn't confined to humans, although, contrary to the old myth, it isn't the elephant that never forgets – it's the dolphin. According to the Severstsov Institute in Moscow, the bottle-nosed dolphin has evolved some tricks few of us could match. One is the ability to put half its brain to sleep while keeping the other half awake. That way it can keep watch for sharks while having a snooze. (One eye remains open.) After about an hour, the dolphin switches brains, sleeping with the other half and waking the sleeping half up.

Dolphin memory matches the very best that humanity has to offer. Even a perfectly average dolphin can listen to a half-an-hour of those high-pitched clicks they use, then play them back *exactly,* including precise click length and pitch.

This is all very well, but you probably don't *want* to memorize the first ten thousand decimal places of *pi* or half-an-hour of high-pitched clicks. All the same, you wouldn't have read this far if you didn't want to make some improvement in your memory.

But before you can really start improving, you need to know how your memory actually works. And to help you do that, here's another list. Read through it just once. Take your time and concentrate, but *don't* visualize or use the locus method you've already learned. The purpose of this list isn't to test your memory or teach you a new system. It's to show you some of the ways your memory works naturally.

How your memory works

So just read through the list once, then cover it over and write down as many words as you can remember, in any order.

```
            Typewriter
            Bird
            Dishwasher
            Truth
            Statue
            Cactus
            Painting
            Persian rug
            Egg cup
            Dictionary
            Lemonade
            Telephone
            Rabid werewolf
            Cat
            Notebook
            Wisdom
            Walking stick
            Flower
            Meaning
            Potted palm
            Guitar
            Pair of boots
            Sports car
            Ruler
            Sheep
```

There are twenty-five items in this list, five fewer than the list you memorized using your home locus. This isn't a test – it's just a way of showing you how your memory works. If you check the words you did remember against the actual list, you'll normally find one or two interesting patterns coming up. These patterns point towards some basic memory principles.

The first is what they call the **principle of primacy**. That's a fancy way of saying you tend to remember more from the *beginning* of a test or a lesson. So you probably remembered *typewriter* OK, maybe even *typewriter* and *bird*.

The second is something called the **principle of recency**. That just means you tend to remember more from the end of a learning session as well. So the chances are your list of remembered words contained *sheep* and *ruler*.

So when you try to remember something without the use of special aids like a locus (or even repetition) the pattern is that you have high recall at the beginning, high recall at the end and a distinct falling off in the middle.

Hunting the rabid werewolf

That's the broad pattern, but there are things that can change it. For example, I'd be prepared to bet you also remembered the *rabid werewolf* even though it comes exactly in the middle of the list where, according to the principles of primacy and recency, you shouldn't be remembering very much at all.

You remembered that particular item because a rabid werewolf isn't the sort of thing you come across all that often. It's also got strong visual associations, which probably popped into your head automatically.

You can impress your friends by referring to the rabid werewolf pattern as the **Von Restorff Effect**. Von Restorff was the scientist who discovered rabid werewolves are easy to remember because they are attention-grabbers. Professional memory experts like Harry Lorayne have long made use of this discovery. If you want to remember something, try to make it an attention-grabber – make sure it's colourful, bizarre, too big, too small, funny or even vulgar.

You've already used the Von Restorff Effect while memorizing that first list using your home locus. Remember the items like the paper clip and the deck of cards? You made them bigger, which was a way of turning them into attention-grabbers. Remember the zebra, which you put on the kitchen table and made tap-dance? Just another way of turning a dull old zebra into an attention-grabber. Remember the postcard? And you probably had no trouble remembering Count Dracula, who is a natural attention-grabber. (Usually by the throat.)

Von Restorff explained

The full Von Restorff Effect is defined this way:

> **'You'll always remember something better if it grabs your attention by arousing one (or more) of your senses or stimulating your emotions.'**

Having created a Von Restorff with the rabid werewolf, the chances are you remembered the items *telephone* and *cat* as well. You may have picked these up almost by association.

Von Restorff shook you awake with his rabid werewolf in the middle of the list, so you automatically paid a bit more attention to words close by.

So much for the words you probably remembered. What about the words you probably didn't? Well, the chances are you didn't recall *truth, wisdom* or *meaning* all that clearly. This is because of a third principle, the **principle of specifics**. Items like wisdom or truth are abstract concepts, not specifics. That makes them hard to visualize, which in turn makes them hard to memorize. Later on, you'll learn how to deal with this problem.

Getting to know how your memory works is a huge help in improving your recall, because you can start to put the various principles to work for you. You'll be coming back to the way your memory works again and again in this book, but in the meantime, you can start using some of the principles you've already learned.

Chapter 4

MEMORY

Your new, improved, portable memory store

One neat way to improve your memory is to *split your study periods*. You'll see why this works if you draw a diagram. Let's suppose you want to learn a list of 40 items. You could represent that list by a line, like this:

First ⟶ Last

You already know your mind has a tendency to remember the first and last items on the list. So you're more or less guaranteed to remember a total of *two* items.

But suppose, instead of trying to remember the whole list, you split it in half, like this:

First ⟶ Last   First ⟶ Last

You're still talking about the same number of words (i.e. 40), but now you've got two lists of 20 words each. If you try to remember one list, then take a break before trying to remember the second, the principles of primacy and recency mean you will remember four items, not two – a 100% increase!

There's a third principle, the **principle of specifics**, but for now, go back to Solomon Veniaminovich Shereshevskii, the man who never managed to forget *anything*. Professor Luria didn't just investigate how good Solomon's memory was – he actually found out *why*. The secret, which should come as no surprise to you, was Solomon's almost unbelievable capacity for visualization.

Solomon could visualize anything. He had a condition called synaesthesia which automatically called up visual associations with sounds, smells, tastes and textures. When, for example, Luria sounded a certain tone, Solomon told him, 'It looks like pink-red fireworks.' When he needed to remember something, Solomon translated it into a visual image and remembered that instead. In his case, the process was entirely automatic, hard-wired into his brain by the synaesthesia. In your case, it probably takes a little effort.

You've already made that effort when you created your first locus to remember the list in Chapter Two. In a moment you're going to create a second locus, which will be of even more use to you because by its very nature you will never be able to forget any of the locations within it.

Your second locus

Your first locus was your own home. Your new locus is you – or your body. It's a wholly portable, mental Filofax you can learn to use in a hundred different ways. To start with, you can use it to make sure you remember everything you have to do today.

Here's how. Assume you have a new list you want to memorize. Only this time, instead of confining yourself to *objects* as in the first list, you're going to start tackling the problem of abstractions – words that are difficult to visualize because they don't refer to things you can trip over or kick. In this case, the abstractions are *actions* – things you have to do on the way home from school.

Your list might go something like this:

> Telephone
> Buy an ice-cream (with chocolate topping)
> Fix the family vacuum cleaner
> Paperback book
> Statue of a frog
> Find out what's showing at the cinema
> De-flea the dog
> Jar of mixed pickles
> Bag of crisps
> Walking stick
> Elastic band
> Top hat
> Doll
> Post letter to uncle
> Pair of scissors

That's a much more difficult list than the first one you tried. Not because it's longer – it's actually a lot shorter – but because it goes beyond simple objects and into the tricky area of abstractions.

But before you start to worry yourself sick about abstractions, let's look at how a body locus works.

First, visualize your body. This shouldn't be too difficult since you're standing in it, but if you're having trouble, go look in a full length mirror. Now…

Imagine the first item of any list on the **top of your head**.
Imagine the next item pasted onto your **forehead**.
Visualize the third item as a neon sign which flashes on and off out of your **eyes**.

Get the idea? You work your way down your body storing item after item from your list.

Item **4** is stuffed up your **nose**. (You can be as gross as you like – you're the only one going to know about it.)

Item **5** goes into your **mouth**.

Item **6** is balanced on your **chin**.

Item **7** can be clearly seen inside your **throat**, which you can visualize as a transparent cylinder.

Item **8** is strapped to your **right arm**.

Item **9** has actually *become* your **left arm**.

Item **10** has been dropped into your **chest**.

Item **11** is tied to your **belly-button** with a big pink bow.

Item **12** is slung low over your **hips** from a belt, so that it flaps and bounces like a Western hero's six-shooter.

Item **13** is sticking out of the **inside of your thighs** making it extremely difficult for you to walk.

Item **14** is now pasted to your **knees**.

Item **15** is under your **feet**.

How to use your second locus

Use your body locus exactly the same way you used your home locus earlier. Visualize the item you want to remember in or on a particular part of your body. Always do this in the same *sequence,* starting with the top of your head.

There's no need to concentrate or try to remember. This locus, like every locus, is a right brain function, so the trick is simply to visualize clearly.

You'll have noticed in this example, that some parts of

your body were transformed into something else – your throat became a transparent tube for instance. You can make the same sort of transformation to any other body part if you find it helps. By doing so you create a Von Restorff Effect and it's an excellent idea to bring in more Von Restorffs elsewhere. Try to get size, number, drama, silliness or vulgarity into your visualizations. If there's a pencil on top of your head, make it a huge pencil, so you're bowed down under the weight. If there's a rabbit in your mouth, make it pop in or out as if your mouth were a burrow.

> By the time you've finished learning the techniques in this chapter, you'll be able to use your portable locus to remember things like album tracks. The pictorial form of the album name goes on top of your head. Pictures representing each track are pasted, in order, through the rest of the locus.

If you've been trying to paste items from your latest list onto your new body locus, you'll have run into the problem of the abstractions by now. How do you work them in?

Working with abstractions

Look a bit more closely at them. As they appear on your list, they are:

1. Buy an ice-cream (with chocolate topping)
2. Fix the family vacuum cleaner

3. Find out what's showing at the cinema
4. De-flea the dog
5. Post letter to uncle

These actions are very different from one another, but they all have one thing in common. Although they're actions, they each involve at least one object. Some of them involve two. If you go through each one, it's easy to extract the objects from the actions:

a) An ice-cream and chocolate topping (two objects)
b) A vacuum cleaner (one object)
c) The cinema (one object)
d) Your dog and his fleas (two objects, unless you count each flea, in which case it gets way out of control)
e) A letter and your uncle (two objects)

Once you start to think about actions, you'll find they almost always involve one or more *things* somewhere along the line.

And here's the secret you've probably figured out already. If you remember the *things* associated with your action, you will *automatically* remember the action you wanted to take with them.

Try it out. You'll find it works. So all you have to do is splosh the ice-cream on your forehead (dripping chocolate sauce onto the carpet) and you're reminded you have to buy one, flash the neon vacuum cleaner out of your eyes and you'll recollect you have to fix it. And so on.

If you use your body locus long enough you will, admittedly, eventually come across a few actions that *don't* involve an object. They're rare, but they exist. You might, for example, want to remember to do your T'ai Chi exercises, which involve you moving in slow motion like

43

an elderly Chinese. How do you cope with that?

You could try remembering by association. There's a T'ai Chi exercise called The Crane, another called Leaping Tiger. So picturing a crane or a tiger might do the trick. But there's an even simpler and more effective way to do it – you visualize yourself *carrying out the action*. You see yourself doing whatever it is you want to remind yourself to do. Then you paste that mental movie onto the relevant bit of your body. When you examine the relevant area of your locus, you'll find the movie will replay automatically.

Remembering longer lists

There's really only one other problem likely to arise with your body locus. There are fifteen locations on the locus, and for simplicity you've worked with a 15-item list. But suppose you want to remember more than fifteen things?

The answer is to extend your locus. You've got two eyes, so you can store an item in each. You've got two nostrils, so you can stuff something up each. Open your mouth wide and count your teeth: you can paste a miniature on each of them ... not to mention your tongue and your uvula (the wobbly bit that hangs down at the back of your throat). You have ten fingers and ten toes, which will more than double your capacity.

You won't be able to extend this locus for ever, but for all practical purposes you'll find it's big enough. Once you start using it, you'll wonder how you ever did without it.

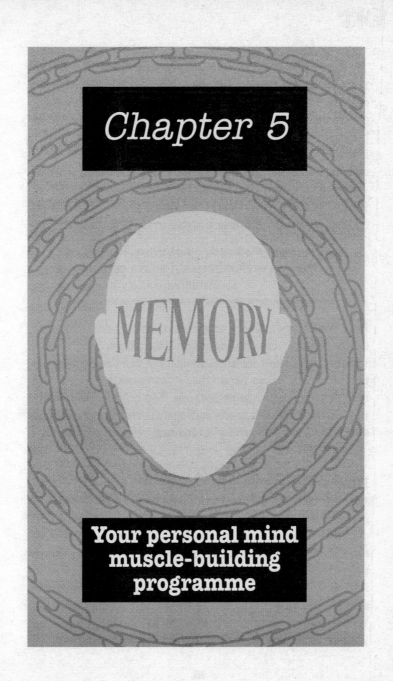

Chapter 5

MEMORY

Your personal mind muscle-building programme

The locus is the oldest memory technique in the world. But it isn't the most useful or the best. It's great if you have a list of things you want to remember, and it does let you impress people by reciting a long catalogue of items forwards or backwards (just reverse the route you take through your locus). But it won't help you remember names, for example, or call out instantly the one hundred and seventy-third item you've just memorized. In other words, its use is limited.

That's not to say you should ignore the locus. It's the basis of a mega memory because it brings in the first principle:

> **You can work miracles if you're prepared to visualize.**

Just about every memory technique is based on visualization or has visualization coming into it somewhere.

But visualization involves more than just *seeing* pictures in your mind. As an experienced day-dreamer, you should be able to imagine sounds as well. You might even be able to imagine textures, tastes and smells. The better you can do so, the more powerful your memory will become.

How well do you visualize?

So how well do you visualize? Here's an easy way to find out. Take the following test when you're nice and relaxed. Find somewhere private, read the first instruction, close your eyes and try to follow it. You'll notice that each instruction asks you to imagine something – not just scenes, but tastes, smells, textures and sounds as well. When you've imagined it as well as you're able, score yourself each time according to the following scale:

Very clear	5 points	☀☺
Clear	4 points	☺
Fairly clear	3 points	☺
Not clear	2 points	☹
Can't do it	0 points	☹

Here comes the test. Try as best you can, eyes closed, to imagine...

1. This book on a shelf among other books
2. Yourself running across grass
3. The taste of a fresh cut lemon
4. The scent of a rose
5. The sound of a galloping horse
6. The feel of tree bark
7. Steam rising from a boiling kettle
8. Yourself lifting a really heavy suitcase
9. Yourself recovering in a hot scented bath after lifting a really heavy suitcase
10. Stepping out of a heated house into the street in the middle of winter
11. The taste of chocolate fudge cake (with whipped cream)
12. A beautiful sunset
13. Your living room at home
14. Being hit with a feather pillow
15. Sunbathing on a beach
16. The taste of cold Coca-Cola
17. Riding your bicycle into a strong wind
18. The smell of coffee percolating
19. The feel of wet clay between your fingers
20. An aeroplane flying low overhead

When you've finished all twenty, noting down your score each time, add up the totals.

75-100	Excellent all-round visualization. You should find mega memory very easy to develop.
40-74	You visualize well and will almost certainly find your ability will improve with practice. You should be able to tackle most feats of mega memory if you're prepared to work at them a little.
Under 40	You could be in a bit of trouble here, but help is at hand. Read on for details of a new system for training your powers of imagination.

If you want to look like Arnie Schwarzenegger, you exercise your muscles. If you want to build up your memory, you exercise your imagination which, fortunately, is a lot easier than weight training. One of the best ways is a little technique developed by the American author Jean Houston for use in her seminars. What follows is a modified version of the Houston technique. To use it, you'll need the help of a friend.

The inner adventure

What you're going to do here is go on an inner adventure. You'll find this a lot of fun – so much fun you'll probably want to do it again and again. Which is fine, because every time you go on an adventure of this sort, you'll be exercising your powers of visualization.

The Inner Adventure Technique described in this chapter does more than help your memory. It's a great new way to develop your creativity as well. Try it a few times and watch the results!

To start, you and your friend should sit opposite one another with your knees almost touching. Get nice and relaxed and become aware of your breathing. Now become aware of your friend's breathing and gradually see if you can work it so you're breathing nicely together.

What you're going to do to begin with is challenge each other, in turn, to imagine a whole variety of images. These will start simple, but as you go on, they'll become more complicated.

If you're like most people, you'll find it easier to imagine pictures than smells or sounds. But with some people it's just the other way round. Whenever the sense image is strong, try to imagine it as if it were literally real, as if you were seeing, or hearing, or touching, or tasting the image. Where the inner image is weak, do your very best to imagine it as vividly as possible.

Sight images

You should start with visual images. For example:

Judy: Sam, I want you to see or imagine your own bedroom.

Sam: Got it. Now, Judy, I want you to see or imagine a sunset...

Judy: I want you to see or imagine a skateboard.

Sam: I want you to see or imagine your shadow stretching out in front of you on the ground.

That's how it's done. Now you do it with your friend. Challenge each other with visual images. Use your own, not the ones in the example, and make sure you give each other a few moments to create the image. Bounce it back and forth for about two minutes, then come back to the book for your next instructions.

Sound images

OK, now you can start giving each other sound images. Like this:

Judy: Sam, I want you to hear somebody singing like a rapper.

Sam: Judy, I want you to hear a tractor starting up.

Judy: I want you to hear a saxophone.

Sam: I want you to hear drums.

Now you try it with your own images for the next two minutes, then come back here.

Taste images

Now go back and forth suggesting different tastes to each other:

Judy: Sam, I want you to taste chocolate ice-cream.
Sam: Judy, I want you to taste a nice, crisp, juicy apple.
Judy: I want you to taste a sponge cake topped with minted, dark chocolate mousse and blobs of whipped cream.
Sam: I want you to taste a potato salad with pickles, eggs and mayonnaise.

Try that with your friend now, going back and forth for two minutes with tastes, making them as simple or as complicated as you like.

Touch images

At this stage you can start using images of touch, for example:

Judy: Sam, I want you to stroke your girlfriend's hair.
Sam: Judy, run your hand over the bark of a tree.
Judy: Feel what it's like when you take a very cold shower after you've been playing football.
Sam: Dig for buried treasure with your fingers in stony ground.

Now you do it, using your own tactile images.

Smell images

On now to smell:

Judy: Sam, I'd like you to smell old socks.
Sam: Thanks a lot! Judy, smell bread baking.
Judy: Smell a cow barn.
Sam: Smell ham and eggs cooking.

Moving images

At this point you can start into something a bit more complicated. You're going to challenge each other with moving images, like this:

Judy: Sam, you're walking along a beach and look up to see a giant ice cube falling from the sky towards you. Watch this cube, seeing its different sides as it tumbles down, turning over and over.
Sam: Judy, you're standing in a railway station and a long train rushes past you.
Judy: You're watching a bowling ball as it rolls down the alley and then strikes the pins knocking them all over the place.
Sam: Imagine a circus with trapeze artists flying through the air, clowns tumbling on the ground and a lion jumping through a flaming hoop in the middle of the ring.

OK, go to it for the next two minutes.

Multiple images

On to something more complicated still. You're going to give each other images that involve more than one sense. Read through the example carefully to get the hang of it:

Judy: Sam, you're driving down a busy street in summer in an open car, chewing gum and passing a chocolate factory.

Sam: Judy, you're sitting by a stream with your feet in the water, on your right side holding the hand of a very old man, and on your left side holding the hand of a young child and you're reciting a poem you learned as a child.

Note how these images bring in touch, smell, taste, sound and sight. See if you can create similar complicated images to challenge your partner.

Preparing for adventure

OK, this is where it gets really interesting. In the example that follows, Sam and Judy are going to create a complex image together. They're both going to contribute to it, both going to watch the picture they're making in their minds. This is a lot easier to show you than explain, so read through carefully what happens next.

Judy: Sam, we're on a huge North American prairie. There's tall grass waving in the wind...

Sam: Yes, I see it. To the north there's a range of high, blue mountains.

Judy: Right, and you can see an old trail winding down from the mountain towards us.

Sam: I can see a cloud of dust on the trail, as if something was coming towards us.

Judy: I think it might be a stage coach.

Sam: Yes, it is. As it comes closer, I can see the driver's an old man, but there's a younger man beside him.

Judy: Is there something following the stage? There's a lot of dust. I can see passengers as well now – two women and a young boy.

Sam: You're right. And I think it may be Indians following them.

Do you see what's happening here? You and your partner decide on a starting point – which could be the North American plains, or an African jungle, or just something everyday, like a street scene. One of you starts, and between you, you build more and more detail, and action into the scene.

Now, have a go at making this sort of story together. After you've passed it back and forth about half a dozen times, one of you should say stop, and both of you should then sit silently for about a minute *watching the scene unfold*. You'll actually see this in your mind's eye, you'll see the composite image develop a sort of life of its own, develop its own story, so to speak.

After watching what happens for one minute, tell each other what you've seen, how the image unfolded.

The whole thing should take about three minutes, after which come back to the book.

The adventure begins

All right, now you and your partner should have enough experience to try for the big one – the shared adventure. In this, you share and actually live in the stories you give one another, and you can keep going until you both feel you've got to the end of your own adventure.

You'll need to work out between you where your adventure should begin. But it might be a good idea to pick somewhere exotic, somewhere that interests you, somewhere that a really exciting adventure would be likely to take place. It can be anywhere you like, real or imaginary – the streets of Chicago, the *Starship Enterprise*, Outer Mongolia, wherever you fancy, just so long as you both agree.

Then, to prepare yourself for the adventure, lie down on the floor together, not side by side, but with your feet facing in the opposite direction so that just your heads are side by side.

When you've settled into that particular position, close your eyes and talk back and forth for a while about where you'd like to start in order to find a really brilliant adventure. Take your time about deciding where to start. Five minutes or so should be about right.

Once you've decided, begin by breathing together for a few moments, feeling your breath synchronize, until one of you suggests an initial image to begin your adventure. Then away you go. Have fun!

Except it's not *just* fun. What you're doing here is exercising your imagination. All of it – your ability to see pictures, hear sounds, taste tastes, smell smells in that wonderful world inside your head. It's your story, your adventure, something you make up between you. But the weird thing is, it won't feel like that. As you relax and get into the swing of things, it'll feel as if the story's rolling of its own accord, you'll feel as if it's *happening* to you. That's when you know you're doing it right.

When you get back, you can congratulate yourself not only on a very exciting and enjoyable experience, but also on improving your powers of imagination beyond all expectation.

Chapter 6

MEMORY

The secret of your second memory

Now you know you have two brains, it may not come as much of a shock to discover you have two memories as well. Psychologists describe them as the short-term memory and the long-term memory.

Your short-term memory is the one you work with all the time, every minute of every day. As a demonstration of how you use your short-term memory, multiply 37 by four *in your head*. Go on – it's not that difficult, especially since it doesn't matter if you get the wrong answer. This is a demonstration, not a test.

One way you might have tried this sum is as follows:

Four sevens are 28. Put down eight and carry the two. Four threes are 12. Plus the two you carried, which is 14. So your answer is 148. 37 multiplied by four is 148.

Great if you got it right, but don't go and hang yourself if you got it wrong. Because the point about this whole thing is to ask yourself where you put the two when you carried it.

You multiplied seven by four and got 28. You put down the eight and carried the two. Then you multiplied the three by four and got 12. Then you looked for the number you'd carried over, and there it was – two. Between the first multiplication and the second, you stored the carry-over answer somewhere. The place you stored it was your short-term memory.

In fact, to be strictly accurate, you stored the whole calculation in your short-term memory until you had the final answer. It's just that you were pulling it in and out of storage so fast you probably didn't notice. Except for the carry-over.

Your two short-term memories

Short-term memory is the place you put things you're going to need in a moment, but certainly don't want to keep permanently. Once you've done the calculation, it doesn't matter if you forget the carry-over was two. You've finished with that, thrown it away. All the time, every day, you're popping things briefly into your short-term memory, then taking them out, dusting them off and throwing them away.

If you've stopped feeling worried about the two brains and the two memories, you might be ready to take on board the fact that you've got two short-term memories as well. One is what's called your **sensory** short-term memory. The other is your **working** short-term memory. Lately, psychologists have been trying hard to measure the time-span of these two short-term memories.

The time-span of your **sensory** short-term memory is actually fairly easy to work out because of the fact you watch movies. The big deal about movies isn't who the film star is. The big deal is that they *move* in the first place.

You probably know already that every movie film consists of a long reel of *still* images. Each of those images is just a tiny bit different from the last. In the first image, you see an actress on East 45th Street, New York City. In the next image you still see her on East 45th Street, New York City, but now her right leg is a fraction further forward than it was in the first image. In the next one, it's further forward still. And so on.

When you run the film through a projector, one still image blends into another and what you see is the actress walking. But how does this actually come about?

What really happens in a cinema is that you watch a whole series of still images separated by very brief moments of darkness. In order to see those images as a continuous sequence of actions, you have to hold the first image in your (sensory short-term) memory until the next one comes along. If you didn't do that, you wouldn't see the movement.

Memory span

Based on this – and some other observations – the experts reckon your sensory short-term memory operates for about one tenth of a second.

The time span on your **working** short-term memory is a bit more tricky. But a scientist called Dr Alan Baddeley carried out some experiments to try to put a value on it. The first thing he discovered was that if you're trying to remember words, you'll remember short words more easily than long ones. No surprises there, but the good doctor asked himself *why*. The answer he came up with was that in trying to remember words, you *subvocalize,* which is just the scientific way of saying you repeat words to yourself under your breath.

This habit, which sometimes slides all the way to repeating them *mentally,* goes right back to the way you were taught to read in the first place. Now, of course, it's so automatic you don't even notice you're doing it.

If you take a trip to somewhere like the United Nations where there are people talking at each other in a lot of different languages, what keeps them communicating is a system of simultaneous translations. You may have noticed how politicians at the U.N. all seem to wear headphones. Expert translators are listening to the person who's speaking and pumping a translation into the headphones while the speech is still going on. The translators have to listen to a sentence, hold it in their memory and come up with the translation with only a minimum of delay.

Scientists studying these translators have discovered their natural memory span during this process is between 10 and 15 seconds. Court reporters, who listen to evidence, then transcribe it for the record, show almost exactly the same working short-term memory span. So somewhere between 10 and 15 seconds seems to be about standard for most of us.

Which, of course, solves Dr Baddeley's little problem. Because if you have a set memory span and you repeat the words to yourself mentally, it's obvious that long words will fill up the time faster than short words – so you can remember more short words than long words.

How many words can you repeat to yourself in 15 seconds? As a rule of thumb, you'll find it's somewhere around 48. You can check that out for yourself. Take any passage from this book and read it aloud at a normal pace while you get someone to time you for exactly 15 seconds. Then count the words. You'll find you've read out somewhere around 48.

Talk faster, remember better

Obviously, if you're a slow reader, the figure will be less. If you're fast, you might manage to squeeze in a few more without it dissolving into garble. Which brings me to a really interesting way of improving your memory. Train yourself to talk faster! Daft though it sounds, the research has shown that fast talkers tend to remember just that little bit better – and the business about subvocalizing explains why.

Of course, the fact you can *read* 48 words in 15 seconds

doesn't mean you'll necessarily *remember* them all. Research done as long ago as 1965 showed that if the words are unrelated – or if you're trying to remember random numbers – you're unlikely to remember more than ten if you're only allowed a single reading ... and the *average* recall is only around seven. Once the list gets longer, you start to forget.

It looks at first as if a bit of a contradiction has crept in here. If the research shows you have a working short-term memory of about 15 seconds and if simultaneous translators can carry 15 seconds' worth of information (about 48 words) in their heads, how come most people can only hold 7-10 random words or numbers in their short-term memory?

Another test

The key to the puzzle is that term *random*. Test yourself again. Take a *brief* glance at the next two lines.

AN INEXPENSIVE HOME COMPUTER

76-45872955473-7814-63259814

Now turn the book over, take a pencil and paper and write down those two lines from memory, one below the other. The question is, which did you find easier to remember?

It's no real contest, is it? The first line was easy. The second line was just about impossible. Yet both those lines contained exactly the same number of symbols – twenty-five. In the first line you had twenty-five letters of the alphabet. In the second you had twenty-five numbers. So how come you found the first line so easy while the second line was so hard?

The answer is, the first line had *meaning*. The letters of the alphabet were arranged to form words and the words painted a familiar picture. The second line had no meaning at all. It was just a string of random numbers with a few dashes scattered to break them up a bit.

If we go back for a moment to the amazing Solomon Veniaminovich Shereshevskii, the Russian journalist who never forgot anything, ever, it's interesting to learn that one of the ways he remembered things was to give them meaning if they didn't already have it.

Remembering nightmares

Take the following nightmare formula, which meant as little to Solomon as it does to most people:

$$N. \sqrt{(d^2.x^{85}/_{vx})} \sqrt{(^{276.86}x/_{n2v_{\pi}264})} \, n2b = sv \, (1624/322).r^2s$$

Even his amazing powers of visualization weren't quite enough in the face of that complexity. But Professor Luria discovered Solomon added meaning to his visualizations by making up a little story.

First, he turned the initial letter N into a man named Neiman. Then he visualized the following sequence of actions:

Neiman came out and jabbed at the ground with his cane, leaving a little round mark which looked like the dot after the N in the formula. He then looked up at a tall tree which was growing in the shape of the square root sign ($\sqrt{}$).

Solomon next imagined that Neiman said to himself, 'No wonder the tree has begun to expose its *roots* – after all, I built two houses here.' A house, in Russian, is a *dacha,* so the d^2 stood neatly for two houses in Solomon's mind. Had he been English or American, he would probably have visualized two dogs, or two dolls, or two daisies and amended his story accordingly.

Once again Neiman poked with his cane in Solomon's story, leaving the necessary (.) mark. Then Neiman said, 'But now the houses are old – I shall have to get rid of them.' This decision enabled him to cross them out in his imagination, leaving him with the next symbol of the formula, the X.

And so the story went on, with Solomon imagining how much he had paid for his houses (**85,000** roubles) and continuing to dream up meaningful pictures which he then added to his story. The end result was a far cry from Tolstoy, but the sequence helped him remember the formula. In fact, as Luria discovered, Solomon could *still* remember it fifteen years later ... by reciting the same story.

Solomon's method for learning this complex nightmare works for simpler scientific formulae as well. When you have one that you need to learn, try making up a nonsense story to take in the various elements in the same way Solomon did.

Chapter 7

MEMORY

A daisy-chain to fill your head with facts

Work on short-term memory has led to the development of a nice little trick for improving your recall. This trick is called chunking.

Chunking means grouping information together in manageable quantities – bite-sized chunks. Most of us already know something about chunking, since it's one of the more popular ways to remember phone numbers.

Suppose you had to memorize this long international phone number:

00441712844474.

Put that way, it looks almost as difficult as the INEXPENSIVE HOME COMPUTER number in the last chapter. But the chances are you wouldn't put it that way. Like everybody else, you'd break it up in chunks, like this:

0044-171-284-4474

You would then concentrate on learning each chunk. First you'd learn the international code for Britain from Ireland, which is 0044. Then the area code for the part of London where the publisher operates, 171. Then you'd split the number itself into two manageable chunks, 284 and 4474. Once you'd learned the individual bits, you'd put them together and end up with the complete number.

This little trick doesn't stop with phone numbers. Professor Aitken, the Scot who memorized the first 1,000 places of *pi,* used chunking as one of the techniques to help him do it.

The secret of successful chunking

Actually, there's a bit more to chunking than meets the eye. One of the many psychologists who's made a study of short-term memory is Dr George Miller of Harvard University. Like just about everybody else, Dr Miller discovered that your short-term memory was limited in the number of items it could hold. Like everybody else, he found the number of items the average short-term memory could cope with was seven.

But then he noticed something the others hadn't. He noticed it was only the *number* of items that was important, not the amount of information in them. What this comes down to is that if you're asked to memorize a list of words without using the special techniques in this book, you will be able to recall up to about seven without too much trouble, but will start to make mistakes thereafter. But if you're asked to remember a list of *sentences,* you'll *still* manage about seven before your memory starts to fall apart.

Obviously there are limits to how far you can take this, but even if your sentences are only five words each, chunking your list has increased your recall from seven words to 35, a very worthwhile increase.

The amazing peg technique

An even more useful trick – one which you've been quietly learning as you've worked your way through this book – is the clothes-peg technique. The clothes-peg technique is very easy to explain:

> **If you can't remember something, peg it onto something else you can.**

If you've worked on the exercises so far, you've already pegged items onto rooms in your home and onto bits of your body. Your next step is to *peg them onto each other*. Once you do this, you can forget all about loci and concentrate on filing memories in such a way that each one actually helps you remember another.

> **Pegging helps you keep track of things that go together. The name of the singer and the name of the song, for instance, or the name of the director and the name of the movie. To keep them both in your memory, peg them together.**

Interestingly enough, when you start pegging in this way, you're moving towards the way your mind naturally stores information. Here's an illustration of the way it works:

One day you're out for a walk in the country. You're looking at a sheep in a field when a red sports car, driven too fast, careers around the corner, blasts its horn and zips so close it blows your wig off.

While all this is going on, your mind is busy filing away memories. Remember Dr Penfield and his slim little electrodes – your mind files away everything, every minute of your waking day. At the time we're talking about, the memories include the sheep in the field, the smell of honeysuckle in the hedgerow, the colour of the car that nearly killed you, the particular sound of its two-tone horn and the feel of your head without the hairpiece.

Your memory isn't logical, Mr Spock

The filing system your mind uses isn't logical. It doesn't pop the sheep into a mental compartment labelled A for ANIMAL or put the sports car into L for LUNATIC. What it does is file the lot together in such a way that *everything is automatically associated with everything else.*

As far as we know, *all* memories are filed by association, but some memories are more strongly associated than others. What strengthens the association is emotion. If something amuses you or gives you joy or scares you witless, it will be more strongly associated with its fellow memories.

Since the sports car scared you witless, it means that from then on, any one of the individual memories – the particular sound of a car horn, for example – will tend to recall the others. 'That reminds me,' you'll tell your grandchildren as they try desperately to sneak away, 'That reminds me of the time the sports car nearly killed me. It was a summer's day and the honeysuckle was blooming in the hedgerow...'

Fear and forgetting

Sigmund Freud, the founding father of psychiatry, discovered a mental process called repression. With repression, you actually work to forget certain experiences because they're just *too* scary, or sad, or embarrassing to deal with. If the business with the sports car fell into that category, you'd very soon forget all about your brush with death. But the associations would still be there, because that's the way your mind filed them.

So, even though you've repressed (forgotten) the incident, sheep will tend to make you see red (the colour of the car), which will in turn remind you of the smell of honeysuckle, which curiously recalls the sound of a car horn. In other words, you've forged a daisy-chain of linked ideas that makes no sense unless you know the circumstances that linked them.

You can examine a few of these daisy-chains for yourself by putting a couple of your friends through what's called a **word association test.** Ask them to tell you the first word that comes into their head when you say the word *mother.* Then feed back the word they give you and ask them what comes into their head when you say that. In a couple of minutes, you'll have a whole long daisy-chain to look at. The dialogue might go something like this:

'What do you think of when I say the word **MOTHER?**'
'**Father.**'
'**Father?** What does that make you think of?'
'**Hat.** He always wears a hat.'
'What does **hat** make you think of?'
'**Coat.**'
'**Coat?**'
'**Fur.**'
'**Fur?**'
'**Tiger.**'
'**Tiger?**'
'**Millicent Hutchinson.**'
And so on.

But even though you start with exactly the same word, you'll get a totally different daisy-chain from everybody you try this one on. That's because everybody forms different associations. But if the associations themselves vary, the *method* of association is exactly the same for everybody. And once you know the trick, you can use it to form associations of your own, which you can then use for miracles of memory. Because when you've made your own daisy-chain, all you really have to remember is the first link, which is all you need to drag the whole chain out.

The link system of memory

This system is called (oddly enough) the **Link System of Memory** and you will be delighted to hear you *already* know most of what you need to make it work.

The locus method showed the best way to get something into your memory was to *visualize*. Pictures are far easier to remember than anything else. You found out that if you visualized something larger than life, remembering was easier still. And if you made the picture dramatic, funny, silly, vulgar or in some other way appealing to your emotions, remembering was a doddle.

All these things are part of the link method, but the heart of the method is association. Even on its own, you can rely on association to make a dramatic difference to your memory. A psychologist named Gordon Bower tested subjects on 12 pairs of words which they had only eight seconds to learn. About a third of the pairs were remembered. But when the subjects were told to create a visual association between the pairs, that simple trick alone sent the scores skyrocketing to 80%.

And association isn't even the whole of the Link Method. Here's another list, so you can try it:

Hill
Trout
Portrait
Stool
Orange
Can of baked beans
Serpent
Sickle
Glasses
Kitten
Key
Earphones
Couch
Rug
Jacket

Fifteen items. For simplicity, the list is only of specifics rather than actions or abstractions, but you know how to deal with non-specifics now and those techniques will work just as well with the link method as they did with the locus method.

How to make a daisy-chain

To turn those fifteen items into a daisy-chain, start with the first, which is *hill*.

As you already know, it's no good filing away the *word* 'hill' – words are hard to remember. What you have to do is file away a mental *picture* of a hill. The exact mental picture is up to you, but could be a silly hill, or a funny hill.

Don't spend a lot of time on your visualization. All you need is a quick, clear mental picture. Hold it in your mind for a second, then go on to the next stage.

The next stage is linking your picture of a hill (which you now remember) with the item second on the list, a *trout*. The link you make between *hill* and *trout* should be dramatic, exaggerated, ridiculous. Anything, in fact, that involves your emotions and grabs your attention.

What sort of association can you make? Any association works, so you *could* make a mental picture of a trout lying beside a hill. But for the best possible results, your association should be direct. You might, for example, visualize a hill of fish, a huge heap of trout as high as Everest. If the fish were wriggling, you've got in movement. If they were smelly, you've involved another of your senses. If they were shocking pink trout all wearing ballet skirts, you've made it ridiculous.

While these example associations will work fine for you (try them!) they won't work half as well as links you *create for yourself*. That's because we're working with *your* head, not mine, and you know better than anybody what strikes you as funny or ridiculous.

Now you have to create a link between *trout* and *portrait*. It should be easy. How about a portrait of the trout sitting up in a high-backed chair, wearing period costume and a three-cornered hat? Just remember, the ridiculous link you make for yourself will work even better.

OK, now you've got a hill that reminds you of a trout and a trout that reminds you of a portrait. Your daisy-chain has got three links.

For the next link, you need to find a ridiculous association between a *portrait* and a *stool*. Maybe the way to go is to see yourself sitting down on a three-legged portrait ... and ripping right through that valuable painting.

In each case, you make the links of your daisy-chain by pegging the new item onto the thing you already remembered. *If you can't remember something, peg it to something you can.* Then you should be able to keep pegging – and remembering – almost indefinitely.

The principles of daisy-chaining

Here are the *basic principles* of a successful link.

Principle 1   **Make it
                          BIG.**
                    Make it exaggerated.
                    Get it out of proportion.

Principle 2   **Make it active.**

Remember that. When you want to remember an action rather than a thing, you can run a mental movie in your head. But the fact is, you can always remember a thing better by having it star in an action movie anyway. Movement is good, action is better and ridiculous action is best.

Principle 3   Increase the numbers.

If you're trying to remember the *serpent* on your list, don't just visualize a link with *one* serpent – wheel in a dozen, or a hundred, or a thousand.

Principle 4   Substitute

This is the most popular principle. When a link was needed between the hill and the trout, it was easy to make a hill out of a whole heap of trout. Substitution is often the easiest way to make a really ridiculous association. It's pretty silly trying to unlock a door with a kitten.

When you've gone through the whole list, turning it into a daisy-chain, test yourself on how well you remembered it. Once again you may not be absolutely perfect on your first attempt, but you should do at least as well as you did the first time you used a locus, and you'll probably do a whole lot better.

Incidentally, you'll find it very useful to examine the few items you *couldn't* remember. What associations did you use? Chances are they weren't ridiculous enough, or exaggerated enough, or big enough. Improve your associations and try again until you have the entire list in your head. And just like the locus system, you will find it stays there. Hours, days, even weeks later, all you need do is remember the first item on the list and you can haul in the entire daisy-chain.

But suppose you forget the first item on the list…?

You can always put one more link at the start of your daisy-chain and associate the first item with the place, person or circumstance you plan to meet up with when you need to remember the list.

Chapter 8

MEMORY

The reasons why you manage to forget

Even as you read this, scientists are hacking their way through the research jungle trying to find out how the brain stores memories. The best guess to date is that short-term memory is an electrical process, a bit like the RAM in your personal computer. Switch off the juice and you've lost everything you had in there. Long-term memory is much more like your hard disk. The scientists currently think it involves chemical changes in the brain, possibly even changing certain proteins.

The reason they think this is that if you're pumped full of drugs that influence the *electrical potential* of your brain, it screws up your short-term memory, but leaves long-term memory intact. Change the prescription to drugs that work on brain *chemistry* and you start developing problems with long-term memory.

Both the electrical and the chemical potential of your brain vary according to the time of day, part of what is called your circadian daily rhythm. This means, almost certainly, that there are times of the day (maybe even night) when you remember things more easily than at others.

Unfortunately these times of day seem to vary with the individual and there's no formula that will let you calculate them for yourself. But it could be worth your while to try to spot them by trial and error. Keep a diary of your study habits and make a note of any time when remembering came easily. After a while, a useful pattern should emerge.

Meanwhile, let's move on from short to long-term memory, if only because we still haven't fully answered that question in the very first chapter. Given, as Penfield discovered, that your brain files away absolutely everything you've ever seen, heard or experienced, how come it's so easy to forget stuff?

The real answer to that lies in the way your memory works. First, Dr Penfield is quite right when he tells you that your brain records absolutely everything. Since he did his experiments, it's been shown repeatedly that subjects under hypnosis can recall the tiniest details of their distant childhood, right the way through to the pattern on the wallpaper.

Your unconscious record

But this recording process is not just automatic, it's also unconscious. You don't know you're doing it, you have no real control over it. Maybe more to the point, you habitually record stuff you will never ever want to remember. But the fact remains that there is a deep layer of your mind where your whole life is recorded, but it doesn't look as if this data was ever *meant* to be retrieved. Unless Dr Penfield gets you, it's unlikely that it ever *will* be retrieved.

The normal process of memory, consciously noting things for recall later, seems to take place on top of this layer. It involves both short and long-term memories and works in three stages.

Stage 1 is called encoding. When you see or hear something new, it drops automatically into your short-term memory and stays there, as you know, for about 15 seconds. If it interests you, you will then make an active effort to transfer the item into your long-term memory. You may do this consciously, as when you want to learn some fact in preparation for an exam. Or you may do it unconsciously, as when you first heard the facts of life and they stuck even though you didn't try to learn them off by heart.

Either way, the transfer process from short to long-term memory is what the psychologists mean when they talk about encoding.

Stage 2 is the actual storage of the facts in your long-term memory. Most psychologists see this as quite separate from encoding, others aren't so sure. They think encoding guarantees storage, but the effort you put into it makes a difference to Stage 3.

Stage 3 is recall. Recall is exactly what it sounds like – the ability to dredge up a specific bit of information from your long-term memory when you need it.

Yet another list!

Here's another one of those interminable lists to help you experience the difference between the three stages involved in memorizing something:

Whale
Pen
City
Bicycle
Shoe
Cathedral
Wool
Tobacco
Holland
Crow
Power point
Abacus
Pebble
Island
Ghost
Goldfish

Read over the list twice (no locus, no link method) then cover it up and write down as many of the words as you remember. Once again it doesn't matter how many you get right, because this isn't a test of memory.

Now, split out the three stages.

When you read the list through twice, you were transferring the words from your short-term memory to your long-term memory. In other words, you were encoding.

Now see how you did on Stage 2, the storage, which tends to happen automatically once you encode. Uncover the list and have a look at it. Do you recognize each word as appearing on the list as you read it a couple of minutes ago? Unless you have the feeling that you're reading some of those words for the first time, then quite clearly they have stuck in your memory. The encoding led to automatic storage.

This is a subtle and difficult point. If somebody prompts you about something and, having been prompted, you suddenly remember it, then it's obvious the memory was in your data banks all the time – you just couldn't recall it. But if you are prompted and *still* can't remember, then it's probably safe to say the information never got stored in your long-term memory in the first place.

So now, you can see the importance of Stage 3. Stage 3 is recall, the ability to get back the information you stored. If you compare the list of words you remembered with the list in the book, you can work out how efficient your recall proved to be.

It's recall that counts

Which brings us to this vital point:

> **When you want to improve your memory, concentrate on getting the memory back.**

What we normally think of as remembering – the storage of information – is automatic when it comes to getting the info in these. But that's no use to you if you can't get it back out again.

So how do you go about getting it back out? Imagine you're introduced to a dull young man in a floral waistcoat. You remember the waistcoat, but thirty seconds later you've forgotten the bloke's name. Why?

For the answer, you need to turn to the man who would drop $1,000 if he ever did that – the man who *never* forgets a name: Harry Lorayne. Harry says most people don't forget – they just never take the trouble to remember in the first place. Which is a very neat way of saying they didn't bother with Stage 1 of the memory process. They made no effort whatsoever to *encode* the information they'd been given. They didn't try to transfer it from their short-term memory to their long-term memory.

When you were introduced to the young man in the floral waistcoat, you probably didn't make the slightest effort to remember his name. You just weren't interested.

Without flicking back, you would probably be hard put to recall the first sentence of this book. You read it all right, maybe not so very long ago, but you've forgotten it now because you didn't make an effort to remember.

> **Most people don't forget – they just
> never take the trouble to remember.**

Remembering requires effort. That's probably the second most important memory lesson you'll ever learn. But it's only the *second* most important. The *most* important lesson is that the effort has to come when you're *filing away* something in your memory, *not* when you're trying to recall it later.

No sweat when you do it right

This is just the reverse of the way most people do it. They sweat bricks trying to recall something if it's important, but make no real effort to try to remember it in the first place. The techniques in this book are all about ways of filing away things you want to remember. Get that right and recall will be no trouble at all. But you have to make the effort in the first place. No system works if you can't be bothered to apply it.

Having said that, there are often good reasons why you fail to transfer information from your short-term memory to a more permanent storage space. As an illustration of this point, read the following passage very carefully because there'll be questions later:

You are driving a train between the suburbs and the city and you start the journey with one hundred passengers.

At the first stop, three passengers get off and twenty-three new passengers get on.

The train travels another mile to the next station where ten people get off, but only five get on.

At each of the next three stops, ten people get off and five get on.

By now the train is approaching the heart of the city so that at the next stop twenty people get off and ten get on.

While still some distance from its destination, jammed points divert the train into a siding where it is forced to halt for seventeen minutes.

Towards the end of that time, ten passengers become impatient and leave the train to walk.

When the points are fixed the train continues on its way with one more stop before reaching its destination.

At this stop, fifty passengers get off and ten get on.

Three questions

Three questions, which you should answer without re-reading the above passage. The first is, how many people were left on the train when it reached its final destination? The second is, how many stops did the train make?

But the third question is the most important: which of the first two questions did you find easier to answer?

You were probably able to make a stab at the first question, but found the second very difficult. The reason why is that the whole test was structured so you'd decide the number of people on the train was important. If you fell for it, this made you *take an interest* in the numbers getting on and getting off. Maybe you even counted in your head as you went along.

But there was nothing to suggest the number of stops was important, so the chances are you didn't bother to count those. So the first question proved a lot easier than the second.

Either way, the memory key was the same. If you took an *interest*, you tended to remember. If you didn't take an interest, you forgot.

To underline the point, here's one more question. What was the name of the train driver?

Without checking back, take a pen or pencil and write it in the space below.

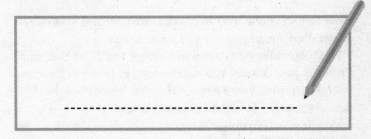

Not easy. Even if you expected a question about the number of stops, the one about the driver was definitely a curler. Without paying attention, it was very difficult for you to remember the name of the person driving the train. You may even think this is a trick question. The first time I tackled that test, I was fairly sure the driver was never named. Which is true enough, but you still know the name all the same.

Read the first five words of the passage again. They tell you quite clearly that the train driver was *you*. The name you should have written down was your own.

Observation test

Here's your last test for this chapter. Have a look at this mini poster:

Now turn the book over and write down what it said on the poster. Don't read on until you've done this.

Did you remember to write down the X at the end? Probably yes. But did you also remember to put in the extra 'is'? The poster *doesn't* read 'He who hesitates is lost!' It actually reads, 'He who hesitates is is lost!'

Very few people notice the extra word. That's because the saying is familiar. It lulls you into letting your attention slide away.

The trick about transferring information into your long-term memory is to keep up your **interest** and **attention.** You should literally *force* yourself to take interest and pay attention at the crucial early stage.

It's a real pain at first, but the good news is that it eventually becomes a habit which isn't easily broken.

Part Two

MEMORY

Advanced Memory Techniques

Chapter 9

MEMORY

How to remember nightmare numbers

You probably won't believe this, but if you're a deep-sea diver, the best place to memorize something is underwater.

The research that produced this little gem was carried out by Dr Baddeley, whom we've already met, and another Cambridge psychologist named Dr Duncan Godden. They took a group of forty divers, split it in half, and tried to teach each half some forty unrelated words. One half had to do the memorizing on dry land. The rest donned their diving gear and did their lessons underwater.

The divers who memorized the words underwater (and were tested on them underwater as well) did almost twice as well as their colleagues who stayed ashore.

What does this mean for the rest of us? One thing it means is that you should try to do your memorizing in familiar surroundings. This isn't always possible, of course, but if you're forced to exercise your memory somewhere strange, try to make sure you're relaxed and comfortable when you do it.

Where you try to memorize something is called its *context*. When Professor Luria tested the amazing Solomon Veniaminovich Shereshevskii, he found that Solomon could not only remember the items being tested, but could also recall details of the room in which he had memorized them.

Flashy

Solomon wasn't the only one to manage this. There's a system of language teaching based on something called flash cards. The idea is that words in your new vocabulary are written singly on cards, which are then shown to you for very brief periods (flashed) while you sit like an idiot and hope to heaven the system works before your holiday starts.

The idea behind flash cards is that they bypass the conscious mind. They're flashed so quickly you simply don't have time to learn what's on them in the normal way.

> **There's an even better way to learn a new language than flash cards. You'll find out about that in Chapter Ten: Never forget another name.**

Flash cards work, but the psychologist R.N. Shiffrin discovered they work even better than you'd imagine. His subjects not only learned the new words and their translations, they could also tell him the size and colour of the letters on the card. Some of them could even tell him what he was wearing when he flashed the cards.

All this is the same mechanism as featured by Solomon Veniaminovich Shereshevskii and the deep-sea divers, the mechanism of context. A comfortable, memorable, interesting, stimulating context will help you remember.

But there's another way to define context in relation to memory. This is the context of the information itself – the context of the stuff you're trying to remember.

Brain teaser

Here's an interesting brain teaser for you.

There was a New York executive whose office was on the fifteenth floor of the building where he worked. Each weekday morning, he would get into the elevator, go directly to the fifteenth floor and begin his work.

At the end of every day, he took the elevator to the ground floor, and went home.

Every second week the executive had to work Saturdays, and once a month he had to come in to work late in the evening too and do two hours overtime. On those occasions he would take the elevator only as far as the tenth floor and would climb the remaining five floors to his office.

The question is, how do you explain the executive's odd behaviour?

It isn't all that easy to figure out. The first thing that springs to mind is that he must be some sort of health freak. He takes the stairs because he needs the exercise. But why only on Saturdays and at night time? And why does he never walk *downstairs* whatever day it is?

The reason this puzzle is so tricky is because it's (deliberately) missing its *context*. You're not told the whole story. If you were, you'd know the executive was a dwarf. Because of his diminutive stature, he could only reach up as far as the button for the tenth floor.

Weekday mornings this didn't matter, because there were always other workers in the lift who could push the right button for him. But at weekends and at night, the lift was almost always empty, so he had to ride as far as he could (the tenth floor) and take the stairs the remainder of the way. Coming down was no problem. If he could reach the button for the tenth floor, he was certainly insufficiently vertically challenged to reach the button for the ground floor.

Context is important when you're doing a jigsaw puzzle. It's twice as hard without a picture on the box. Context is also important when you want to memorize something. If what you want to remember forms part of a broader picture, then overviewing that broader picture and understanding the principles involved will make your memorizing easier.

Primitive principle

This is a memory principle so fundamental it's primitive. When you visit a city for the first time, you learn your way around by noticing landmarks. In this way, you pick up the broad geography of the city, then you start to fill in details by relating them to the landmarks you already know. The landmarks establish the context that helps you remember where you are. You recall your favourite pizza place is 'over by the British Museum' or 'just beyond the Empire State Building'.

The way you do it isn't so far removed from the way an Australian Aborigine finds his way through the Outback. He looks for the broad context with its (often subtle) landmarks and visualizes an overview map which he keeps in his head. When he goes walkabout, he compares his physical surroundings with the mental context map and avoids getting lost.

The question of context is very closely related to the question of *meaning*. In some experiments carried out in 1975 volunteers were asked to try to remember new words in three different ways. The first way was to try to remember the look of the word. The second was to try to remember its sound. The third was to try to remember its meaning.

No prizes for guessing which they found easier. The volunteers who were trying to remember meanings scored a 71% success rate. That was more than twice as good as those working on remembering the sound (29% success) and nearly five times better than those who concentrated on the visual appearance. They managed only a miserable 15% success.

If you understand the context, if you understand the meaning, your encoding procedure – shifting the item from short-term to long-term memory – will *automatically* improve.

But what do you do when you have to remember something that has *no* context, something that has *no* meaning? What do you do when you have to remember rotten little *numbers*?

Although your brain became fully functional at the age of five, it was only about 90% adult size. It continued to grow until about the age of ten. That finished its purely physical development.

Side by side with the growth of your physical brain, you went through specific well-charted stages of mental development between the ages of 6 and 8, with another spurt between 10 and 12. If you're a girl, your brain development at the age of 11 was something like twice that of boys your own age. But don't let your brain go to your head, because by 15 the boys have more than caught up.

Your mega brain

Around the age of 16, whether you're male or female, you are, in brain terms, fully grown and well able to make a nuisance of yourself. At that stage, you have, like the rest of us, the capacity to remember the equivalent of $2^{10,000,000,000}$ binary bits of information.

There's not a lot of point in trying to spell out how vast that figure is. But it's a lot of memory – more than enough to record your entire life, as Penfield discovered … with capacity to spare.

So you've got more than enough memory for tricky stuff like numbers. Yet most people find anything longer than three or four digits out of the question. Numbers have no *meaning* and for most of us very little *interest.*

Go back to the two-line test you did earlier with the INEXPENSIVE HOME COMPUTER. The second line of that test was:

76-45872955473-7814-63259814

Take out the dashes, which were only there for show, and you have 7645872955473781463259814. If your life depended on memorizing that number within the next five minutes, you might start to feel a bit nervous. But all the same, you will soon be able to memorize that – or any other twenty-five digit number – well within the five-minute limit ... provided you're willing to do some preparation.

Although Hideaki Tomoyori can recite the value of *pi* to 10,000 decimal places, this does not actually involve his memorizing ten thousand different numbers. The number *symbols* he has to recall are only ten – 0, 1, 2, 3, 4, 5, 6, 7, 8, 9. His real problem is getting them in the right order. This may sound a shade simplistic, like telling you your only problem in climbing Everest is to put one foot in front of the other. But bear with me, because the basic difficulty in remembering numbers lies with those ten digits. Unlike the letters of the alphabet, they do not convey specific meanings when you combine them. And as things in themselves, one is very much like the other.

Now you *can* go some way towards memorizing numbers by chunking, but there are limits to how far chunking can take you.

You might think of placing gigantic cut-out versions of

the numbers in your locus. You'll do better this way than trying to learn by rote, but probably not all that well. The daisy-chain method doesn't work with numbers either.

The problem, as you've doubtless discovered, is that visualizing single digits is no fun. There's not much you can do to make them interesting. But cast your mind back to the principle you learned for the link method:

> **If you can't remember something, peg it to something else you can.**

Memory monks

There are a couple of excellent ways to do this. The first is based on the fact that monks don't forget their prayers.

There are a number of reasons why this is so. They're talking to God, for one thing, which means their prayers are very important to them. They repeat them frequently for another – monks talk to God a lot. But the third factor, which comes up in every monastery of every religion of the world, is that monks, as often as not, chant their prayers. They do this because rhythm and rhyme are fantastic memory aids.

You'll be able to find out more about rhythm later. For now, just take a look at rhyme.

Monks aren't the only ones to use rhyme as a memory aid. You probably used it yourself when you were learning the number of days in each month of the year. And when somebody asks you how many days there are in October, don't you *still* chant something like this:

Thirty days hath September,
April, June and November.
All the rest have thirty-one,
Save February which has twenty-eight alone.
Excepting, though, one year in four,
When February has one day more!

Sure you do. As poetry, it's a long way from Wordsworth, but it certainly helps you remember.

So one way to peg the ten basic number symbols to something useful is to find ten things that *rhyme* with them. Fortunately somebody started making those rhyming associations for you when you were still in the nursery:

One, two ... buckle my shoe
Three, four ... knock at the door
Five, six ... pick up sticks

And so on...

That little rhyme gives you immediate associations for the digits

2 ... shoe
4 ... door
6 ... sticks
8 ... gate

Number associations

So, you've *already* got nearly half the necessary associations and it shouldn't be too difficult to find rhymes for the others. Let's start with the hardest, which is 0 (nought or zero). You might try *caught* if you call the digit 'nought' but you'll find something easier to visualize a lot better. So forget nought, call it zero and rhyme it with *hero*.

One (1) is easy for anybody who enjoys food. Make it *bun*. Two you already have as *shoe*. Three could be *tree*. Five rhymes with *hive,* seven with *heaven* and nine with *wine*. If you've got better rhymes, use them — you don't have to stick to the ones suggested. As you know from making links, your own associations are always best.

Here's the whole list:

0	hero
1	bun
2	shoe
3	tree
4	door
5	hive
6	sticks
7	heaven
8	gate
9	wine

This list is actually all you need to handle numbers in your memory, but you might find it useful to add one more item: 10 = *hen.* You can, of course, *create* 10 by adding together the bun and the hero, but 10 is such a useful number it's very handy to have a single visual symbol. The 'big fat hen' of the nursery rhyme is perfect.

By now you know it isn't the *word* you should associate, but the *picture* it conjures up. Use the link method you have already learned to make this easy. Visualize the digit zero being lifted by a brawny *hero* – somebody like Conan the Barbarian. Now see the digit one with a large mouth chomping on a *bun*. And the digit two pulling a *shoe* onto one of the feet it grew specially for the occasion.

As you go through, make the pictures as clear, interesting, humorous or vulgar as you can. See a tall, bushy *tree,* a stout wooden *door,* a busy bee-*hive*, a pile of *sticks*, an angel leaning on a signpost to *heaven*, a red-painted, wrought-iron garden *gate,* and a bottle of the very finest vintage *wine.*

And one by one, associate the pictures with their appropriate numbers in any way that really appeals to you. If you don't like the ones used here, dream up pictures of your own. As you know, when making links, your own associations are always best.

The difference between this list and the others you worked on is that you aren't memorizing it just to pass a test. The list itself is a memory tool that will help you remember numbers in all sorts of situations in the years ahead. So work on it until just *thinking* about the digit brings up the right pictorial association, and just thinking about the association brings up the right digit.

Once you get the hang of the number system in this chapter, remembering dates becomes a piece of cake. Since dates on their own aren't usually much good, use the link method to peg the date you remember to whatever happened on that date. Before you know it, your history grades will double.

The rhyming method works for most people but there is another set of pegs based on the shapes of the digits themselves. With that system, you take a long, hard look at the shape of the digit and see what it reminds you of.

Picture numbers

Here again, it is what the shape makes *you* think of that's important, so your best bet is probably to work out your own. But for what they're worth, here are the associations given in the book:

0 = an orange
1 = a thermometer
2 = a duck
3 = the moon
4 = a little girl
5 = a rabbit, cymbal or drum
6 = a tuba
7 = a war axe or cliff edge
8 = an hour glass
9 = a tennis racquet or stylized man

You could see the orange, thermometer and even the duck, but does the digit 3 look like the moon? And what about the little girl or the rabbit? But if these sorts of associations work for you better than the rhyming links, go ahead and use them or, as always, make up associations of your own.

Once you have them, here's how they work. First, take the number you want to memorize:

7645872955473781463259814

Next, translate it into visual images, by substituting the pegs you've just learned for the digits themselves.

So 7645872955473781463259814 now becomes:

Heaven ... sticks ... door ... hive ... gate ... heaven ... shoe ... wine ... hive ... hive ... door ... heaven ... tree ... heaven ... gate ... bun ... door ... sticks ... tree ... shoe ... hive ... wine ... gate ... bun ... door

This might not look much better, but now that you have visual associations, you can try linking them together in a daisy-chain, or placing them in twenty-five different locations in your locus. Either way will take you further towards remembering the number than trying to memorize it cold. If you've put in a lot of practice, these methods may even allow you to memorize the whole number first time without a mistake.

But there's a better way.

More chunking

Try chunking. Try splitting the number into more manageable bite-sized chunks:

7645-8729-5547-3781-4632-5981-4

Now, instead of 25 things to remember, you have only seven things (chunks) to remember. Each of those chunks contains four bits of information except the last, which only contains one. So why not try storing *boxes* in your locus, each box containing the relevant items?

The first box, at the front door, would open up to reveal a photograph of little fat cherubs playing harps on fluffy clouds, a bunch of sticks, a door and a hive of bees that swarm out to buzz around your head.

The next box in the hall contains a wrought-iron gate, an oil painting of angels in heaven, a giant shoe and a vintage bottle of red wine. And so on.

If you try this, you'll find it works quite well.

But there's an even better way.

The memory story

Remember the nonsense story on page 63 which included the visual elements associated with the various parts of the mathematical formula? You can do that here. Your story might start something like this:

Just after I died and was on my way to heaven I came across a bunch of sticks some devil had been collecting for firewood and used them to knock on the door so I could get in. Unfortunately this disturbed a hive of bees which swarmed around the gate preventing me from getting into heaven. I beat at the bees with my shoe but this made them angry so I gave them some wine to settle them down and they returned a little drunkenly to their hive.

And so on. As you make up the story, *visualize* it happening. This is what drills it firmly into your memory. If you can see it happening in your mind's eye, you'll automatically remember it afterwards.

Don't use the story above. The one you create yourself will be much more effective. It doesn't have to be great literature – any old nonsense will do, just so long as it helps you remember.

Chapter 10

MEMORY

Never forget another name

Here's a familiar scene. You're at the disco. A friend comes up trailing his nerdy cousin. Your friend says, 'Hey, meet my cousin *Mumblety-mumblety*.' You smile a little and say coolly, 'Hi'.

And you have as much chance of remembering the cousin's name as you have of dating your favourite film star. Memorizing long numbers is sort of fun – and very impressive – but you don't have to do it all that often. Memorizing names is something else. You're meeting new people all the time and it gets embarrassing if you can't remember who they are five minutes after you've been introduced.

Now you can make sure it never happens again by learning how to burn names into your memory so effectively you should never ever forget them. The system is so powerful you'll remember names not just for weeks or months, but years. It really is that good.

But before getting down to the system, write this behind your eyes in words of fire:

> **Most people don't forget – they just never take the trouble to remember.**

In the little cameo above, you didn't make any effort to remember the cousin's name. You didn't even *hear* it properly. The music was loud, your mind was on other things, your friend was speaking quietly, so the name just slipped right past you.

How do you expect to remember something you didn't even *hear*?

Make sure you hear the name

Long before you get down to special systems, that's the first secret of remembering names. Make sure you hear them in the first place. If you don't, ask to have the name repeated.

Lot's of people think that's rude, but it's not. You're not going to remember something you never heard in the first place, so you *have* to ask to hear it again.

Having asked for the name to be repeated, make sure you really do try to shift it from your short-term memory (which is a 15-second-long black hole) to your long-term memory. In other words, *make an effort* to remember.

One way to do that is to use the name. Forget cool. Forget the casual wave and the glazed look and the mumbled 'Hi.' If you want to remember, get that name into your reply. Put on the glazed look, give the casual wave and mumble, 'Hi, Pete' or 'Sam' or 'Kimberley' or whatever the name was.

If you want to make really certain, repeat the full name, which you can do in the form of a question: 'Hi, Kimberley. Did Jim just say you were Kimberley *Foster*?'

Having made sure you've heard the name, fed back the name and asked confirmation for the second name, your next step is to *repeat* the name. Try not to overdo this or you'll end up coming on like a politician, but make the effort to slip the name into the conversation from that point on: 'Do your friends call you Kimberley or Kim?' That sort of thing.

Just those three things – making sure you hear the name, feeding back the name, and repeating the name – will guarantee you don't forget it right away.

How to burn names into your memory

But if you want to burn it into your mind for ever, here's what to do next.

Let me introduce you to the people pictured on pages 112-116.

No. 1 is Eric Tyson.
No. 2 is Queenie Braithwaite.
No. 3 is Ulrika von Gottenfurter.
No. 4 is Pamela Wein.
No. 5 is Maurice Maeterlinck.
No. 6 is Slobodon Brichkoff.
No. 7 is Paul B. Wallace.
No. 8 is Eileen Holmes.
No. 9 is Terence Goldblaum.
No. 10 is Rosaria Piezovic.

They're very different to look at, but they all have one thing in common: their names are murder to remember. If you can remember names like these, names like plain, old John Smith will be a cinch.

So, how do you do it?

For a start, don't panic about spelling. Names like Piezovic, Maeterlinck and Brichkoff may be difficult to spell, but you're not trying to spell them. Here comes the first secret:

> **You're trying to remember the *sound* of the name, not the spelling.**

Once you get that into your head, even the most exotic name becomes a little less terrifying. In fact, by concentrating on the *sound,* you'll soon find you can remember exotic names even more easily than plain names.

So Step 1 is to *listen to the sound of the name*.

Step 2 is going to sound very familiar. Step 2 is *convert the name into a picture or pictures*.

Remembering names is no different from remembering anything else. You can do it the hard way by concentration and repetition. Or you can do it the easy way by engaging the right brain and making pictures.

But what sort of picture springs to mind with Ulrika von Gottenfurter?

Take the name apart

Well, let's take it apart and find out. It might be difficult to picture anything when you hear the name *Ulrika*. But listen to the sound. Two syllables: *ul* and *rika*. Neither syllable carries a meaningful picture in its own right, so try for something close.

The closest you might get to *ul* in English is *owl*. The closest you might get to *rika* is *wrecker*. So Ulrika's first name becomes 'Owl Wrecker'.

The *von* bit of Ulrika's name would tell you in Germany or Austria that she's a posh girl, but that's no help in remembering. So instead of *von* substitute *van*.

Using the same approach, split up *Gottenfurter* into its basic components. They sound like Got en furter. Which is very close to 'God Hen (frank)Furter.'

Put them all together and Ulrika's name becomes Owl Wrecker Van God Hen Furter. It looks pretty odd written down, but it has one enormous benefit over the original. It's a whole heap easier to visualize. All you have to do is glance at those words and you'll have a series of pictures consisting of an owl, a demolition (wrecker) van, God in

His long white robes and long grey beard, a hen and a (frank)furter.

> **Pulling difficult names apart like this works just as well for foreign words. So when you're trying to learn a new language and you're having difficulty, try breaking down each new word the way you're learning here, and pegging the result to the meaning of the word.**

This may sound a bit complicated, but try doing the same job on the others. Remember, each and every time you're converting the *sound* of the name to what for you is its nearest pictorial equivalent.

1. Eric Tyson: Hair Rick Tie Son. Which translates pictorially into hair, a rick of straw, a necktie and a young boy.
2. Queenie Braithwaite: Queen Knee Breath Weight.
3. Ulrika von Gottenfurter we've already done: Owl Wrecker Van God Hen Furter.
4. Pamela Wein: Palm Wine. (That one was easy.)
5. Maurice Maeterlinck: Morse (as in Morse Code) Meter Link.
6. Slobodon Brichkoff: Slobby Don Brick Cough.
7. Paul B. Wallace: Pole Bee Wall Ace.
8. Eileen Holmes: Eye Lean Homes.
9. Terence Goldblaum: Tear Wrench Gold Bloom.
10. Rosaria Piezovic: Rose Aria Peas o' Vetch.

Those breakdowns will work for you, but if you take the trouble to make your own breakdowns of these (or any other) names you'll find they work much better. Here's a short list you can practise on. First, say the name aloud to get the sound, then break it into its components, then list down the nearest pictorial version of those components:

Alistair Bonfield
Celia Houlden
Thomas Mapstone
Caroline Priestley
Gail Thornberry

Sometimes, of course, you don't have to break the sounds down at all. *Gail* in the practice list above could instantly become *gale,* meaning a great storm. Names like *Smith* or *Harper* carry their own pictures – a blacksmith and a musician playing a harp. Remember, it's the sound not the spelling you're dealing with. *Sheppard,* once you sound it, instantly translates into a picture of a shepherd. Play around with the practice list, making the best sound to picture associations you can, then try doing the same with friends' names for a while. When you've done that enough to be comfortable with the process, come back to the book.

Now make the link

Your next step is to take the pictorial components of any given name and link them together. You can use the daisy-chain method you learned in Chapter Seven, or make up a little action scene combining the link method with the story method you use to remember numbers.

If all else fails, you might like to try using the pictures singly, without linkage. The most difficult name on that first ghastly list only brought up six pictures. All the rest were just three or four.

Now you've got your pictorial versions of the names you want to remember, you're ready for the third and final stage of this system. For that you need to study the *face*.

We'll start with face number 1.

1. This distinguished gent is Eric Tyson. But for the moment forget about the name, even forget the pictorial version of the name you've been working out and concentrate on Eric's most prominent and distinguishing feature – it's that amazing handlebar moustache. It's the one thing that really jumps out when you look at his face.

Now make your pictorial associations by visualizing the moustache.

Your pictorial associations with this name could be Hair Rick Tie Son. Try putting that together into a funny fantasy scene which shows a hairy hay-rick tying up a small boy using a necktie. (This way you have the double benefit of using *tie* both as a noun and a verb.) This scene is ridiculous, fantastic, exaggerated and stupid, which makes it just about perfect as a memory jogger.

And now, as a final link in the chain, visualize the scene taking place on *Eric's handlebar moustache.*

Once that association's made, sight of the moustache at any time in the future will always tend to call up your silly association: *hairy Rick tying up somebody's son* – and *voilà,* you have the sound of the name: Hair Rick Tie Son! Eric Tyson.

Let's see if it works for the next face.

 **2.** What's this young woman's most distinguishing feature? It's definitely those enormous spectacles, but maybe you should be a bit careful here. If you just want to remember her name for a while, linking to the spectacles will be fine. But if you want to be absolutely sure of a permanent link, you'll have to take into consideration that spectacles, by their nature, are changed every so often. Queenie might dump them altogether in favour of contact lenses. So spectacles could be tricky.

You might do better linking to her fringe, except that here again she might decide to change her hairstyle. So in real life you might be scanning Queenie's face for some other distinguishing characteristic – a mole, big ears, a gap in her teeth, or whatever. But for the sake of remembering her *as pictured,* go for the specs if you want to.

In her left lens (as you look at the picture) you might imagine the *Queen* hoisting her skirt to do a *knees-up.* In the right you could visualize a mouth blowing visible *breath* comprising big, black, one-tonne *weights*. Read the pictures left to right and you've got her name Queen Knee Breath Weight: Queenie Braithwaite.

3. Here's the one that looked so tricky to begin with. What's her most striking feature? You can forget the woolly hat and scarf – she'll take those off as soon as she gets into the warm. But that large mouth will go with her to her grave, so use that as your distinguishing feature.

And right across her mouth you could run a little movie of the owl driving the wrecker van and knocking down God –

being God, He wasn't using the pedestrian crossing – who is accompanied by a terrified hen eating a frankfurter. It'll never star Bruce Willis (Bruise Will Hiss) but it will remind you that this little girl's name is Owl Wrecker Van God Hen Furter: Ulrika von Gottenfurter.

4. This woman's big brown eyes are exactly what you need to carry your associations. Stick a palm tree in one and a bottle of plonk in the other and you'll remember for ever she's called Palm Wine: Pam Wein.

5. No doubting old baldy's most distinguishing feature and no worries that this one will disappear either. So, in order to remember his name for ever, try superimposing the dots and dashes of the Morse Code across the top of his bald patch, sink an electricity meter into his forehead and hang a link of chain from one of the dials. Morris Meter Link: Maurice Maeterlinck.

6. This one is tricky, because his most distinguishing characteristic is undoubtedly his beard, which he could shave off in the morning. But if he *doesn't* shave, linking his name to another characteristic simply won't work, since the beard will always be the first thing you'll notice. So beard it is.

Into the beard goes a dirty, ill-dressed academic – a slobby Don – carrying a brick which has just caught a head cold and is coughing furiously. Slobby Don Brick Cough: Slobodon Brichkoff.

7. This executive type has two possibilities – his close-set eyes and his oversized conk. You could opt for the nose because stuffing things up people's noses is so rude it's bound to be memorable. So a pole goes up one nostril, a bee up the other. Then build a wall on his upper lip like some weird moustache, but a wall of cards rather than bricks with each of those

cards showing an ace of diamonds. Pole Bee Wall Ace: Paul B. Wallace.

8. It has to be the hair, doesn't it? What's really memorable and impressive about this woman is the sheer volume of her crowning glory. That's not going to change for a long time, so you can feel safe making a link to it. This one is simple: a giant cartoon eye leaning on two rather sweet little houses: Eye Lean Homes. Eileen Holmes.

9. This hunk has thick, frizzy hair as well, which raises an important point. There is nothing to stop you using the same distinguishing feature for two or more people. It still works.

But if you use the piggy eyes you can have him weeping huge tears in the form of mechanic's wrenches. This gives you his first name. For the second, simply stick a golden carnation in one of them. Tear Wrench Gold Bloom: Terence Goldblaum.

10. Here again, there's more than one possibility for a memorable feature – you have a choice between her large eyes and her long hair. Either way, the link will involve an operatic rose singing an aria while walking through a meadow full of wild peas and vetch. Rose Aria Peas o' Vetch: Rosaria Piezovic.

That's how you do it. You already know your own associations, your own links will work better every time. But it's also worth knowing that of all the memory systems you've learned so far, this one requires most practice. You have to get used to looking for prominent features, to listening to the sounds in the name, to turning those sounds into pictures, then linking those pictures with the prominent feature.

It's a complicated process and the first few times you try it, you're going to wonder if it's worth the hassle. But the good news is that if you invest the effort at the beginning, the whole thing becomes almost automatic after a while.

When that happens, you stop forgetting names.

More uses for this system

And not just the names of people you meet. You can use the system to remember the name of a historical personality, because it works just as well from an old photograph, drawing, oil painting or sculpture.

There are two interesting things about this. One is that if you start remembering the faces with the names of historical personalities, it makes remembering what they did a whole lot easier. So if you're a history student, life suddenly perks up.

The other interesting thing is that you don't have to know what the historical personality looks like at all. You can visualize a face you think *should* look like him or her and link the name to that. Sounds a daft thing to do, but it does make the whole history lesson easier.

You can also use *parts* of the system for other things. For example, if you want to remember a particularly difficult word – some ghastly scientific term, for example – you can break it down into visual elements just the way you did with the names above, then link these to the meaning of the word.

Other people may not know what you're talking about, but *you* will.

Of course, none of this helps you *spell* the names you hear or write down the scientific terms correctly.

First, getting the spelling of a word wrong often involves the same mechanism as forgetting a name – you don't make the effort to remember in the first place. If you know there's a particular word you always misspell, don't just shrug and tell yourself you always get it wrong, write the word down, look at it and concentrate for a moment on *where* you get it wrong.

Take the word *embarrassment,* for example. You might write that as *embarassment* or *embarrasment* or *embarasment.* They all look much the same, and they're all wrong. But, in the first example, it's wrong at the 'r' (there should be two of them). In the second, it's wrong at the 's'. And in the third, it's wrong at both. Finding out where you're going wrong means you have less to remember, since you can afford to concentrate only on the part of the word that goes wrong, not the whole word.

Find out where you go wrong and visualize yourself writing the word correctly. It won't work miracles like the other systems in this book, but it should help quite a lot.

So should asking people to spell their names (or difficult terms) for you. When they do, write them down if you can, and visualize them letter by letter in your mind's eye. If you can't write them down immediately, for some reason, still carry out the visualization and write the word down later. Every effort like this you make to remember helps burn the spelling into your memory.

Chapter 11

MEMORY

How to detonate a memory bomb

The idea that remembering takes a lot of time and effort has probably been with us since the cave days, but it only got scientific support in 1879. That was the year Herr Doktor Hermann Ebbinghaus made history by carrying out Germany's very first memory experiments.

Dr Ebbinghaus was nobody's fool. Even though the research hadn't been done yet, he realized that things like meaning and visual associations had a huge influence on memory. So he decided his subjects were going to memorize long lists of nonsense syllables.

What he discovered was what we've always known – the harder you try, the more you succeed. He called his discovery the *total time hypothesis* and all teaching methods have been based on it ever since. Grit your teeth, gird your loins, put your best foot forward and, above all, keep your nose to the grindstone. Repeat, repeat and repeat again. The longer your nose retains contact, the more you will remember. That's the total time hypothesis.

You might think the total time hypothesis is a load of tosh, but strictly speaking, this isn't true. As Ebbinghaus found, the longer you spend trying to memorize, the more data you will retain. There is a straight line correlation between the two.

The trick isn't to deny the total time hypothesis, but to try to use it as efficiently as possible. The first thing to realize is that repetition alone just isn't going to hack it. You know that already, but your teachers may not, so you might like to prove it to them ... and yourself.

A nasty little test

The easiest way to do this is to write down, or draw, exactly what appears on both sides of a 1p coin. Without looking, of course. When you've finished making a mess of that little test, ask yourself how many times you've seen and handled a penny. It certainly runs into hundreds and, unless you're very poor, probably into thousands. Yet all that repetition didn't make it easy for you to remember.

The coin test was actually carried out under scientific conditions in the United States in 1979, when nobody performed any better than you just did. Results were confirmed by Dr Baddeley. This study made use of the fact that the BBC was currently in the middle of a campaign to alert the public to a wavelength change. Everybody polled had heard the announcements hundreds of times, but the vast majority had no idea at all what they said.

This isn't, of course, to say that repetition has *no* effect. Advertising people have spent lots of other people's money to prove it does. But repetition only works when you manage to make people interested. With interest, repetition certainly works. Without it, you can repeat until the cows come home and nobody remembers anything.

What it all comes down to is that if you stick to routine ways of remembering – repeating and repeating in the hope that something sticks – the total time hypothesis will stretch for ever. In other words, you'll guarantee yourself a long, hard, boring slog … with feeble results at the end of it.

But if you're prepared to shift gear and engage your right brain with the sort of visual methods given in this book, you'll cut total time to a minimum. You'll also have more fun and your bottom-line results will be nothing short of miraculous.

And let's get one thing out of the way:

You can't clutter up your memory.

This is something that often genuinely concerns people. You show them how to memorize shopping lists and they lie awake at night worrying about how they might confuse last week's list with this week's, or get their locus so crowded there just isn't any more room in there.

Dr Ebbinghaus did some work on this problem as well. He discovered you could actually plot the whole process of forgetting on a graph. If you study that graph, you'll find it follows a predictable curve. What it shows is that if you remember 100% of the things you want to remember in the first few seconds, after about twenty minutes you'll have forgotten about 40% of them. In an hour, more than half of them have disappeared.

Remember, though, that we're talking about the ordinary process of forgetting here, not what happens when you use right brain techniques, or even when you make a massive effort to remember in the conventional way. And so far, the graph shows no surprises. We all know we forget things as time goes on. But as you continue to plot the graph, something interesting comes up.

After eight hours you're remembering somewhere between 30-40% of the total. After 24 hours, you're *still* remembering between 30-40% of the total. The actual figure has dropped a little, but not much. Even after a week, it's still only a little under 30% and that figure hardly drops at all as the week stretches into a month. Thereafter, the Ebbinghaus graph shows you've forgotten about as much as you're going to forget. Anything that's left will stick more or less indefinitely.

So if you leave your right brain alone and don't make too much of an effort with your left, you'll forget a lot over the first hour, but after that it tails off until you more or less stop forgetting altogether. Psychologists working with the Ebbinghaus material have been at great pains to find out why.

The latest research shows your memory is as much like a tree as anything else – a tree where branches produce branches. So far from new memories pushing out old ones, each new memory creates the possibility of additional memory storage, like one tree branch growing another. The more you use your memory, the better it gets.

The reusable locus

So clutter doesn't happen. Your locus is eternally reusable. You can empty it out a million times and it's always ready for more. Your link system is just as wonderful. You can forget a list just as easily as you remembered it, allowing it to fade away when you no longer need it. You can memorize a different shopping list every week for a year and never get two of them confused.

Or you can memorize a whole host of different lists and retain every one. All you need to do is put your mind to it. That lump of folded grey matter inside your skull has more storage capacity than the largest computer ever built.

In many situations, however, just memorizing something isn't enough. You need to be sure you remember to remember.

Take this everyday scenario. You bump into a friend who asks you to tell your other friend Toby (who's in the supply business) that she needs four paper-clips, a floppy disk, half a dozen free-range eggs, a didgeridoo, a pair of pink socks, a ball-point pen, a leather elbow patch and a brass Buddha.

You memorize the list instantly, thanks to your amazing right brain. But there's a problem. It's going to be three days before you get back home. How can you be sure you'll remember this little conversation when you meet up with Toby? You memorized the *list* all right, but how can you be sure you'll remember to tell Toby *about* the list?

The answer's really easy. You set a trigger in your mind that will detonate an explosion of memory the instant you set eyes on Toby.

How to set a memory trigger

This is one of the easiest of all the memory tricks and a very simple visualization. To set your trigger, call up a picture of Toby in your mind and superimpose a huge neon sign flashing LIST on his forehead. Or, if you want to make sure it's the particular list your friend asked for, visualize her sitting on Toby's head. All the old principles apply: make it exaggerated, funny, vivid, action-packed, emotional or rude.

You can even form your daisy-chain out of the list as usual, then link the *first item* – in this case the paper-clips – to Toby. In your mind's eye, just create a ridiculous association, like seeing Toby with paper-clips coming out of his ears.

However you set it, the rest is automatic. Rest easy about the whole thing, because when you see Toby in three days time, your trigger will explode the memory.

If you're always losing your door key, get into the habit of setting a flashing light trigger each time you set it down. Then, when you can't remember where you left it, close your eyes and look for the flashing light. If that doesn't work, buy yourself one of those cute key-rings that answers when you whistle for it.

Triggers are extremely useful. You can set more than one and still be confident they'll all explode exactly when you need them. You might, for example, have to buy six textbooks from the bookshop, groceries from the supermarket, some DIY stuff from the ironmonger's, modelling kits from the hobby shop and a takeaway from the Chinese restaurant. You also have to remember to call at the travel agent's to pick up your ticket to Bermuda.

It would be possible, of course, to daisy-chain one long list and work through it in sequence. But that leaves you with no freedom to mooch about the way you like. Much better to create a daisy-chain for each place you plan to visit, and set a trigger to detonate when you step through the door. That way, you remember what you want at exactly the right time.

A trigger for a trigger

You can even set a trigger to remind you to visit the next place where you've set a trigger. Mentally superimpose the hobbies shop on the supermarket checkout, for example. Or a trigger can be set using a landmark you know you'll pass, or a person you know you'll meet. Triggers can be set using *anything*. One good one is the chime of a church clock. That way you are reminded to do something at a specific time.

In every case, the mechanics are exactly the same. You decide where you want to place your trigger, visualize it clearly, then make a ridiculous link between it and whatever it is you want to remember.

Chapter 12

MEMORY

**Mix 'n' match for
mega memory**

By now you know for certain that the one real key to an excellent memory is visualization. It's visualization that engages your right brain and helps shift stuff from short to long-term memory so effectively it burns it in for keeps.

What may not have occurred to you just yet is that you can mix and match visualization techniques. You can put daisy-chains into your locus. You can peg your locus not just to your body, but to your body when you're wearing specific clothes. You can set triggers in the middle of chains, so you jump from one to another. For all practical purposes, there really is no limit to how far you can expand your memory. You might remember an amazing fact that was mentioned back in Chapter One: you have more brain cells than there are stars in the galaxy. You have so much room in there, you'd have to live for ever to fill up half of it.

One of the most impressive mixtures is when you link the number pegs to items in a list. This allows you to pull off the sort of memory tricks most people believe are simply impossible. Next time you're at a party, you can turn yourself into the centre of attention and get yourself a solid reputation as a Memory Marvel.

Here's how, using the list of thirty items like the one you memorized in the second chapter. Only this time, the list will be just a little different:

1. Canteen of cutlery
2. Diamond
3. Pair of spectacles
4. Walking stick
5. Armadillo
6. Teacup
7. Envelope

8. Leaf
9. Horse
10. Queen Victoria
11. Personal computer
12. Water ski
13. Coil of rope
14. Bomb
15. Cloud
16. Electric plug
17. Tin of beans
18. Seaweed
19. Colt 45
20. Hammer
21. Glove
22. Rowing boat
23. Planet Mars
24. Piece of coal
25. Hell's Angel
26. Crown
27. Bag of chips
28. Cigarette
29. Iceberg
30. Pocket knife

The difference is that the items on the list are numbered. If you memorized that list using your locus or by daisy-chaining it together, how would you feel if you were asked to name the thirteenth item? Or what was the numbered position of the coil of rope?

You could work it out, of course. You could go through the whole list laboriously counting. But surely there's a better way, a faster way?

There is and this is it.

The better, faster way

> Instead of putting your list in a locus or daisy-chaining the items together, link each of them with the visual symbol for its relevant number.

Your first item on the list is a canteen of cutlery. Your visual peg for the number 1 is a *bun*. So link the bun with the *canteen of cutlery*. You can have a cartoon bun eating its dinner with the cutlery. Or you could create a bun-shaped box for the cutlery. Your own associations are best, so work one out and visualize it clearly.

Item 2 is diamond. The peg for 2 is shoe. Maybe you're going to work with a diamond shoe, or maybe you'd prefer to see yourself hobbling round because you've got a huge diamond in your shoe. Make your own association and visualize it clearly.

Item 3 is a pair of specs. You could see them growing up like a tree out of the ground, or falling out of a tree onto your head. Go to it yourself and make your own personal spectacles/tree association.

Item 4 is a walking stick. See yourself opening a walking stick like a door in order to get into the next room ... or whatever picture forms the most vivid, emotional, rude or dramatic association for you.

When you get to item 10, you might take up my suggestion of using the big, fat hen as the peg for that useful number. But what about the pegs for 11, 12, 13 and so on?

The way to handle those is so simple it's almost childish. You create pictures for the numbers larger than 10 exactly the same way you create figures for numbers larger than ten. *You put the basic digits together*.

Here's a list of visual associations long enough to let you handle that whole list. As you read it, count the numbers aloud.

0 = hero	**10** = hen (or bun hero)	**20** = shoe hero
1 = bun	**11** = bun bun	**21** = shoe bun
2 = shoe	**12** = bun shoe	**22** = shoe shoe
3 = tree	**13** = bun tree	**23** = shoe tree
4 = door	**14** = bun door	**24** = shoe door
5 = hive	**15** = bun hive	**25** = shoe hive
6 = sticks	**16** = bun sticks	**26** = shoe sticks
7 = heaven	**17** = bun heaven	**27** = shoe heaven
8 = gate	**18** = bun gate	**28** = shoe gate
9 = wine	**19** = bun wine	**30** = tree hero

This looks quite complicated the first time you see it, but if you've learned the pegs for the basic digits, the rest follows automatically. You won't really have much trouble if asked what *shoe hive* stands for, or *bun gate*, or *tree tree*, even though that last one wasn't on the list.

Link your list items to the relevant pegs (by visualizing ridiculous associations) until you've gone all the way through to number 30: the tree hero pocket knife.

131

Now, even though you haven't used a locus or chained the words together, you can still recite that list from start to finish simply by mentally repeating the numbers 1 to 30 and allowing them to bring up their relevant associations:

One ... bun ... canteen of cutlery.
Two ... shoe ... diamond.
Three ... tree ... pair of spectacles.
Four ... door ... walking stick.

And so on, all the way through the list.

How to impress your friends backwards

If you want to recite it backwards (which impresses people) start at 30, which equals tree hero and is associated with pocket knife. Then go to 29, shoe wine, and so on.

At this stage, pegging the items to the numbers has only helped you duplicate what you could already do using a locus or a daisy-chain. But there's more. Have someone ask you for a specific numbered item on the list. Let's say they ask you for the 23rd. Your visual association for 23 is shoe tree and this peg immediately calls up the planet Mars. If they ask for item 16, you see the peg bun sticks and find the association is an electric plug.

It works just as well in reverse. Challenge a friend to give you any item on the list and you will immediately call out its number.

'Queen Victoria!' calls your friend.

The item conjures up a picture of the monarch nursing a big fat hen. 'Number 10!' you call back.

'Seaweed,' calls your friend.

The item is linked with a bun and a gate. 'Eighteen!' you

call back.

'Bomb!' screams your friend in desperation.

But by now you're incapable of forgetting. The bomb is associated with a bun and a door so you call back at once, 'Fourteen!'

As you grow accustomed to your number pegs, the linkages become easier and easier, hence faster and faster. With practice, you can end up making them almost as quickly as someone can read out a list to you.

Chapter 13

MEMORY

Finding lost objects

You know how it is. You walk into the house, set down your book or your keys or your purse, take a shower or whatever, and the next thing you know, you can't find the stuff you set down. You just can't remember where you put it.

It's easy enough to see *why* this happens. When you set something down, you aren't *trying* to remember where you put it. You aren't making the slightest effort to *encode*. If you've read this far, you'll know that's death on wheels when it comes to trying to remember.

It's no good pretending you can use any of the techniques given so far. They're all conscious techniques and when you set your keys down, you're on automatic, which means the whole thing is unconscious. You may know all the techniques in the world, but you aren't going to apply them.

Does that mean there's no hope in a situation like this? Not exactly.

Scientists have discovered hypnosis can usually persuade you to remember where you set something down. Since you probably don't have a good hypnotist handy, it's useful to know you can manage without one – not quite so well, perhaps, but with luck well enough to find what you've lost.

The trick is to do to yourself what a hypnotist would do to you if he or she were there.

The first step is to relax. Sure you're uptight about losing the keys, but you aren't going to find them by running round like a hen without a head. So sit or lie down comfortably, and go through the relaxation technique given in the next chapter.

When you've got rid of the tension, visualize. Visualize, in detail, exactly what you were doing when you lost the object. *Don't* concentrate on the object – that'll lock you up. Concentrate instead on remembering in as much detail as you possibly can exactly what you were doing between the time you last had the object and the time you realized it was missing.

You got off the bus. You walked up the street. You opened your front door (so you must have had the keys then). You came into the hall. You kicked the cat. You walked to the kitchen. You were feeling peckish. You put the keys on the dresser. You opened the fridge. You found the triple chocolate fudge whirl your folks were trying to hide from you. You —

Hey – *You put the keys on the dresser!* That's how it works. As you go through the sequence in detail, the visualization drags up the memory of what happened when you set the keys down and where it was.

The point about all this is what you learned right at the beginning of this book. Everything you do, everything you see and experience, is *automatically* stored in your memory. It doesn't fade, it doesn't vanish (short of brain damage) ever. So when you mislay something, the trick is to pull out the memory of when and where you set it down. Relaxing combined with sequential visualization helps you do just that.

Chapter 14

MEMORY

The fourteen
study secrets

MEMORY

You now know pretty well everything there is to know about visual, right-brain memory. But you'll notice there are still a few more pages in the book. That's because there are still a great number of ways to improve your recall without ever bothering your right brain. What they amount to are study secrets – ways of tackling what you want to learn so that you get the greatest possible return for the least possible effort.

Once you know these study secrets, you can use them in conjunction with the visualization techniques you've learned to turn yourself into a sort of power swot – somebody who absorbs knowledge like a sponge.

The first secret is going to knock you out:

Make sure you make mistakes

We live in a world where everybody's into *success*. Which is fine, except that all the attention on success has stopped people thinking straight about *failure*. Almost everybody thinks failure has something to do with making mistakes.

But failure isn't about making mistakes. It's about not managing to do something. This may *sometimes* involve making mistakes, but it could equally well involve lack of energy or illness or even simply changing your mind about what you really want.

Mistakes are part of being human. They're inevitable … and useful. They're probably the most useful learning tool there is. The first study secret forces you to face the fact that you *will* make mistakes. It goes further. It encourages you to *welcome* mistakes so you can learn from them. In the old days, Americans liked to say, 'The person who never made a mistake never made anything.'

140

This doesn't mean you should ignore mistakes. Correct them, learn from them, then forget them. The more often you do, the further you'll go. And you'll be a lot more relaxed about your performance, which is a benefit as well, as you'll see later.

The business about mistakes applies to study generally, but it's specially important when you're dealing with memory. The Bulgarian psychologist Dr Georgi Lozanov ran a test to discover how many words of a foreign language students could learn in a day. What he found was fascinating.

When the lessons set out to teach a maximum of 100 new words a day, students managed to remember 92 of them – i.e. their success rate was 92%.

But if the number of words they were required to remember was doubled, the success rate actually went up – to 96.8%. Doubling the words to learn doubles your chances of making a mistake … yet the success rate rose.

Doesn't that tell you something about making mistakes?

Just to hammer the point home, you should know about Lozanov's second finding. When the students were asked to learn 1,000 words a day, their success rate dropped … but only from 96.8% to 96.1%. It was *still* far higher than when they were trying to learn just 100 words a day.

The second study secret is:

Don't butterfly

Of course you have a lot of things to do, but research shows that if you move randomly from one study project to another, your retention goes to bits.

In order to achieve maximum recall from your super

memory techniques, plan to work your way completely through one project before starting on another. But don't try to do it at one sitting. That runs contrary to the third study secret coming up.

Study secret number 3 is:

Take breaks

You can thank the French psychologist Henri Pieron for that bit of information. His research showed that however well your study process was going, your overall retention improves if you take a break every half-hour. The break itself should be about five minutes long – you get no benefit from increasing it, and you lose study time.

   Don't cheat on yourself. Each break *must* be a complete change from study. Switching from learning German to solving an equation in calculus just doesn't hack it.

The fourth study secret is my favourite:

Eat

Odd though it may sound, there's a definite relationship between munching and memory. The reason for this is *blood sugar*. Blood sugar is exactly what it sounds like – the amount of sugar in your blood. Blood sugar rises after a meal, drops when you get hungry. The feeling of hunger is actually your body's signal that blood sugar is getting low. That's why sucking a sweet will usually banish hunger as quickly as a full meal.

   If your levels of blood sugar drop too low, your

concentration nosedives and your memory blows a fuse.

You can trigger a fast, dramatic rise in blood sugar (and put on a ton of extra weight) by eating cake, sweets, chocolates, most breakfast cereals (which tend to have sugar added), drinking a whole variety of soft drinks, or by taking sugar direct – as glucose sweets or as spoonsful in your tea.

Unfortunately, blood sugar raised in this way doesn't stay high long. Sudden jumps in blood sugar levels trigger your body to produce insulin which burns the sugar out, sometimes leaving you worse off than when you started.

So snacking while you study is obviously a good idea, but the *type* of snack is important. Anything that contains refined sugar will give you a quick lift, but won't hold high levels long. Fruit is better, but best of all is a *protein* snack. This raises blood sugar levels more slowly than cake or fruit, but keeps them higher for far longer. In other words, it helps you maintain your best possible memory performance throughout the whole of your study period.

You get protein in things like peanuts, soya products, lentils, meat, poultry and fish.

The fifth study secret is:

Review your work

After every ten minutes of study, review your work for five minutes. In other words, read through it again quickly, concentrating on the important points. Give it another five-minute review after a day, then further three-minute reviews at the end of each week, month and six months. This sounds like hard work and it is ... until you make it a study habit, at which point it becomes second nature.

143

The suggested pattern of review is based on much experimental research and should lead to a boost in your recall of anything up to 500%!

The sixth study secret may be surprising:

Don't smoke

Research in the States has shown that people who don't smoke have a 24% better level of recall than those who do. British research strongly suggests that smoking adversely affects the *length of time* you can remember things as well.

This has almost certainly got something to do with oxygen levels in the brain. Your brain is an oxygen-driven machine. While it accounts for only about 2% of your body weight, it routinely consumes a massive 20% of the body's total oxygen supply. Smoking cuts down the volume of available oxygen, hence the efficiency of your brain.

Oxygen is behind the next study secret as well.

The next study secret, number 7, is:

Take exercise

Lack of physical exercise doesn't seem to affect how well you remember something, but it does slow down the time it takes for you to recall it. Here again, we're probably talking about brain oxygen levels, which improve with exercise.

The best time to take the exercise is immediately before an important study period, or immediately before you need to recall the information – e.g. in an exam. But don't exercise *too much*. You'll see why in the next secret.

Study secret number 8 is:

Don't study when you're tired

And obviously try to avoid taking tests in that condition too. Tiredness plays havoc with your concentration, which in turn wrecks your memory. You may feel you should push yourself to learn, especially in an emergency situation, but while it makes you feel like a saint, it's counter-productive. If you really want to boost your memory, take a little nap.

The ninth study secret is:

Dream on

Everybody tells you to get enough sleep when you're studying. That's good advice, but for an unexpected reason. There is a proven relationship between memory and *dreaming*: the more dreams you have while you're asleep, the better your memory works when you're awake. The research was done by Dr Chris Idzikowsky at Edinburgh Hospital.

Scientists (and anybody else) can tell when you're dreaming by watching out for REM. REM stands for Rapid Eye Movement and if you watch a person sleeping (or a cat or a dog, come to that) you'll easily spot the flicker behind the eyelids which indicates they're having a dream.

All sleep is important to memory, but since REM sleep is most important of all, it's useful to know that your first period of dreaming doesn't start until about an hour and a half *after* you fall asleep. You'll typically dream for about ten or fifteen minutes, then sink into dreamless sleep until the end of your next ninety-minute cycle.

But, as the night goes on, your dreaming periods get longer, while the time between them shortens. So you do most of your dreaming in the morning hours before you wake up. Knowing this pattern helps you keep your memory well tuned. Setting the alarm clock early may gain you an extra hour or two of study time, but only at the expense of memory.

Secret number ten is:

Organize your material

This one is really sneaky, because the simple act of organizing your material seems to transfer it *automatically* from your short-term to your long-term memory. In other words, if you get the material organized, you'll end up remembering just about as much from the organization as you would if you'd tried to learn it without organizing.

It was a Canadian who discovered that one. Dr Endel Tulving, a psychologist working at Toronto University, took two groups of students and handed each student in each group a pack of 100 cards printed with 100 different words – one word per card. One group he told to memorize the words. The other group he told to sort the words into categories.

Tulving tested both groups after they'd completed their jobs. The organizers remembered just as many of the words as the memorizers.

Your next study secret, number 11, is really pleasant:

Relax

Tension blocks memory. If you've ever had a name or a fact on the tip of your tongue, you know the last thing you can do is force it. Relax and think of something else, and the chances are it'll pop right into your head.

Having said that, relaxation needs practice, especially if you want to be able to relax in a high-stress situation – an exam, for example. If you can bear it, set aside a short period every morning from now on for the practice of relaxation. As little as ten minutes is well worthwhile, provided you practise *regularly*.

Sit in a comfortable chair. If you lie down on a couch or bed, you'll fall asleep. Make sure you're sitting comfortably. Rest your arms on the arms of the chair and have your legs uncrossed. If your folks ask what you're doing, give them a mysterious smile and tell them everybody needs a little rest.

Start by taking three deep breaths. As you do so, put your hand on your belly button. If your abdomen swells under your hand, you're breathing properly. If it's just your chest that moves, you're breathing shallow and need to learn to take in more air.

Tibetan yogis, who use breathing techniques, talk about pot-breathing, because if you're doing it right, your stomach and abdomen take the shape of a pot. Teach yourself pot-breathing by sticking your stomach out each time you breathe in. This draws air into the *bottom* of your lungs.

(If you really want to do this properly and happen to have a cassette recorder, you might like to record the following instructions and then carry them out as you play them back.)

147

Having taken two or three pot breaths, take another and hold your breath for the count of three. Then let your breath out slowly to the count of six. As you do so, mentally repeat the word relax, and notice that when you breathe out, you *relax* a little bit more.

Next, take another deep breath and hold your breath to the count of five. Let it out even more slowly to the count of ten. Again, as you do so, focus on the word *relax.*

Now close your eyes, breathe shallow and easy, and let go of all the thoughts that have been racing through your mind. You're going to focus on relaxing various muscle groups throughout your body. Notice the different feeling in each muscle as it relaxes.

Start with your hands. Relax your fingers and thumbs. Let any tension trickle away. No tension now in your hands or wrists.

Let the relaxation spread up from your hands into your arms and elbows. Focus on the word *relax* and feel yourself growing more and more relaxed.

Move on to your upper arms and let those relax.

Next, concentrate on relaxing across your shoulders and between your shoulder blades, letting go of any muscle knots and tension. Now move down your back and let all the tension go.

Bring your attention to your neck and let any tension here drain away as well. Remember always to focus on the word *relax.*

Becoming more and more calm and relaxed, bring your attention to any tightness in your scalp and face. Remove the tension from your forehead, eyebrows, eyelids. Let all the tension drain away from around your eyes, allowing yourself to become even more relaxed.

Let the tension drain away from around your mouth and lips. Move your teeth slightly apart, then relax your chin, jaw and throat. Remember to breathe steadily and easily, relaxing more and more with each breath out. Unwinding, letting go, growing more and more deeply relaxed. By now you should be feeling very calm and peaceful.

Allow the relaxation to move down to your chest, loosening and relaxing any knots or tightness. Feel the muscles of your tummy relax completely.

Now the relaxation moves into your thighs and drains out all tension from your thighs and knees. Then let the relaxation spread into your legs, your ankles, your feet and toes.

Continue to let go a little more, so you grow more and more calm, comfortable, peaceful and relaxed. Enjoy the sensation of relaxation for a few moments, then open your eyes.

Nice, wasn't it? If you use this technique regularly, you'll very soon train yourself to relax anywhere ... and thus improve your recall.

Study secret number 12 is:

Ask yourself questions

This simple technique isn't very well known, for some reason. Most people will advise you to study by reading and re-reading the material over and over.

This is OK advice, but only just OK. A far more efficient approach is to read the material, then *ask yourself questions about it*.

This not only helps you remember the material, but it also pin-points those areas where your understanding or recall is weak. That way you can review and revise far more efficiently.

Lucky study secret 13 is:

Keep your study periods the same length

If you alternate between long and short periods of study, you will remember less than if you divide your study time up into (at least roughly) equal periods.

Finally, study secret 14 is:

Study for one hour per day

Back in 1978 a research programme showed people who studied one hour per day learned twice as fast as those who studied four hours a day, broken into two two-hour sessions.

Obviously you have to apply this one sensibly. You may be up against deadlines or facing such a volume of material that you simply have to study more than an hour a day. But if you aren't, an hour a day is the most efficient period.

Chapter 15

MEMORY

Five hidden patterns that will help you remember

Even outside of the study secrets, the way you approach what you study can make a big difference to what you remember – and how much you understand. This goes back to the way your mind works. If you know the basic shape of something, you remember it more easily.

Interestingly enough, everything you read in a textbook has a basic shape. That's because there are only so many ways a writer can present information. The good news is that just five basic shapes crop up time and time again. Learn to recognize these shapes and you'll automatically absorb more of the information in them.

Here are the patterns you should look for:

The Step Pattern

This is the easiest to recognize, because it's the simplest. Authors often make it even more obvious still by labelling it for you. You must have lost count of the number of times you've seen something like this in a book:

Step 1: Take a piece of square paper and fold it across both diagonals.

Step 2: Fold the corners in towards the middle.

Step 3: Turn the folded paper over and crease horizontally.

Step 4: Throw it away and buy yourself a hamburger.

This is, of course, the Step Pattern of presenting information. The material is fed to you in clear-cut stages, one building on the other. If Step 4 hadn't become a stupid joke, the instructions above would eventually have taught you how to fold a model of a Chinese junk out of the single square of paper.

The Step Pattern doesn't have to be as clearly labelled as the example above. The individual steps don't even have to be numbered. Just watch out for information presented in clear-cut stages, each stage adding to the last, and you've found yourself a Step Pattern.

The Aspect Pattern

The Aspect Pattern approaches information by breaking it down into bits and presenting one after the other. Like the Step Pattern, it can run to any length.

You'll find the Aspect Pattern crawling over any encyclopaedia you care to consult. Here's an example from the *Grolier Electronic Encyclopedia:*

Great Britain, history of

The story of the British Isles is that of a creative mixture of peoples. In modern times their insularity gave these islands security and enabled them to influence the world...

Island peoples to 1066

Various peoples of different stocks entered Britain in the early stages of its history. It is convenient to call them, from their speech, Celts and Anglo-Saxons...

Romans

The Roman occupation of Britain illustrates this division. Present in England from AD 43 to c.400, the Romans were effectively confined to the lowland zone. Many signs of those four centuries of occupation can be seen today...

Germanic Settlements

Even before the Roman withdrawal, immigration of the Germanic peoples from across the English Channel and North Sea had begun…

Norman Conquest

The Vikings, or Norsemen, raided all around north-western Europe and made their most important settlement across the English Channel in Normandy…

And so on, all the way up (yawn) to the

Welfare State

The end of the war in 1945 brought to power the first majority Labour government. Britain already had a system of old-age pensions and health and unemployment insurance…

You have only to look at this example for the Aspect Pattern to become clear. The article moves from a brief overall introduction to Aspect 1, which was the appearance of the Romans, then Aspect 2, the Germanic invasion, and so on.

It's easy to see this pattern in encyclopaedias, because they tend to use subheads. But it's not all that hard to spot the Aspect Pattern even when there isn't a subhead in sight.

For example, imagine you've read a boring article on the Welsh landscape which takes you through its geographical relief (Aspect 1), soils and drainage (Aspect 2), climate (Aspect 3) and finally vegetation (Aspect 4).

The Problem Analysis Pattern

The Problem Analysis Pattern which comes up a lot in discussion documents looks like this:

Problem → Effects → Causes → Solution.

As an example, you might examine the Analysis Pattern in this sequence:

Problem: Tim has a flat head.
Effects: It makes it difficult for him to attract girls.
Causes: Too much yoga.
Solution: Buy a hat.

OK, that's not a serious example. But how about this:

Problem: Reports of UFO sightings by airline pilots are increasing.
Effects: People are becoming nervous about the possibility of alien invasion.
Causes: Increased air travel.
Solution: Investigate the problem instead of denying it exists.

Quite obviously, that example is stripped to its bare bones so the pattern itself is clear. The whole thing would include statistics on UFO sightings, interviews with people who claim to have been abducted by aliens, a discussion of causes which might be extended to include the nature and origins of the aliens, and a selection of solutions such as plans to capture a saucer. What would result might be a 10,000 word essay, but if you read it with an eye to pattern, it's the Problem Analysis Pattern that would emerge.

The Scientific Pattern

This is a three-stage pattern often found in scientific works – hence its name. It looks like this:

Thesis ➔ Evidence ➔ Conclusion

The thesis is a particular idea which doesn't have to be true, but may be worth looking at.

Thesis: time travel is bound to be invented one day.

Now, in this pattern, you look for proof.

Evidence: fossil shoe prints have been found dating back to the Jurassic era – long before there were any people on the planet.

Once the case is presented and proved (or refuted) you then draw your conclusion:

Conclusion: there may be time travellers among us today, heavily disguised.

The Propaganda Pattern

This pattern looks much like the Scientific Pattern. Here's how you tell them apart:

The Scientific Pattern puts forward an idea, and sets out to find out whether or not it is true.
The Propaganda Pattern puts forward an opinion and tries to persuade you to believe it.

The Propaganda Pattern is another three-stager. It looks like this:

Opinion→ Persuasion→ Recommendation

As an example, the pattern might begin with the opinion that Donald Duck should be the next Secretary General of the United Nations.

You might persuade me to believe this with the arguments that ducks don't start wars and the old quack isn't likely to cut back on international medical aid programmes.

The recommendation is obvious – vote for Donald.

There you have the five most common patterns when it comes to presenting information. But knowing the patterns isn't enough – you have to find which of them is in the material you're studying. Once you do that, the material takes on a familiar shape that's easier to understand.

**If it's easier to understand,
it's easier to remember.**

Sometimes, of course, you'll find information that *isn't* presented in any of these five patterns. When this happens, decide which of the five patterns suits it best and reorganize the information in that pattern. Hard work but, here again, the effort you make will help your understanding, so you'll remember it better.

The only thing the patterns *won't* help you with is concentration. Concentration follows interest, which is why you probably find it easier to concentrate on the biography of your favourite pop star than the history of an accountancy firm.

Unfortunately study often involves trying to remember facts about things that *don't* really interest you at all. Visualization helps because while the facts remain dull, you can still have fun with the pictures. But the real bottom line, unfortunately, is practice. Although you have to force yourself to begin with, the longer you do it, the easier it gets.

Chapter 16

MEMORY

Key words that make remembering easy

You may have the idea that when you're studying, you should, ideally, try to remember everything you read. Not so. Outside of fiction, the whole art of effective writing is to relate any new material to *what the reader already knows.*

This means there's no such thing as an article or textbook containing 100% new information. You wouldn't understand it if there was.

Check this out for yourself. Go to your library and find/ask for something advanced on the mathematical arguments against Einstein's initial presentation of his Unified Field Theory. Unless you're a physicist, you can read the work from cover to cover and *still* know absolutely nothing. The writer obviously knows his subject inside out, but has failed to communicate that knowledge to you.

This is not to fault the poor old author. Every writer assumes a specific level of knowledge in the reader. If it isn't there, then the whole of the book contains new material and becomes bewildering. The information has nothing to relate to.

One expert concluded that the ideal balance in a book was 20% new ideas related to 80% familiar material. His research showed most readers loved this mix and books that got it right became popular.

What it amounts to is that, when you're studying, you can cut down on what you need to remember by as much as 80% ... and still hold onto every last scrap of new information in the book.

The gold prospector's secret

The secret is to approach your next text book like a prospector in the Old West. You know there's gold in them thar hills, but you might have to do a lot of digging to find it. Decide in advance what you want to learn, then search out the new information that helps you. This way, you avoid wasting time on diversions.

And if you use your right brain memory systems with the fact-extraction method coming up, you can end up remembering the essentials of just about any subject under the sun. That makes the approach ideal for exams. It needs a bit more work than some of the techniques you've learnt, but the results are worth it.

Let's assume you want to learn about the search for life in Outer Space. There's a lengthy article about it in your encyclopaedia. How do you go about extracting and remembering the essential information?

First, read right through the article ... but don't try to remember any of it. All you're doing is getting an overall picture. When you've done that, read through it again, this time looking for the basic *pattern*. (If you need to, refer back to Chapter Fifteen for a refresher on the five basic patterns you're likely to come across.) Since it's in an encyclopaedia, there's a good chance it's the Aspect Pattern. If not, figure out which pattern does apply.

The keyword secret

Now comes the latest memory secret. Once you have the pattern, start looking for *keywords*.

A keyword is a single word that stands for a whole block of information. For example, the SETI (Search for Extra Terrestrial Intelligence) programme involves scanning the sky with radio telescopes for intelligent signals from the stars. The keyword here is *radio*.

But when you start to study the subject, you'll find the

search for life isn't confined to intelligent life. There have been experiments conducted on the surface of Mars to find out whether there are any microbes present in the soil. Scientists are also interested in two of Jupiter's moons which have conditions just about tolerable to life as we know it. Keywords here are *Mars* and *Jupiter.*

Work your way through the information like this, selecting the keywords for each block of information you want to learn.

When you've done this, it's time to put your right brain into gear. List your keywords, then turn each one into a picture. Things like *radio* and *Mars* are easy, but a word like *SETI* isn't. Treat it exactly as you did the names in Chapter Ten. *SETI* might remind you of the settee in your sitting room, giving you a nice easy-to-remember picture.

Now all you have to do is daisy-chain the keywords. When you need to know something about life in Outer Space, your daisy-chain will let you move step by step through the article.

Sometimes the keywords are all you'll need to remember the content. But sometimes they'll only help you with the broad structure. You'll need something else to help you retain the facts.

Facts coming out your ears

Just about everything you're expected to learn bristles with facts. Madame Curie discovered the properties of radium. The world's greatest ever explosion occurred in Siberia. The square on the hypotenuse of a right-angled triangle equals the sum of the squares on the other two sides. But it's often not enough to know the facts – to understand them, you have to relate them to other things.

For example, Madame Curie's work on radium had implications for medicine (it killed her), physics (she had discovered radioactivity), politics (who's got the biggest bomb?), military strategy (who's got the biggest bomb?) and history (Hiroshima).

The world's greatest explosion seems to have been caused by a meteor or small comet plunging into the Tungusta region of Siberia. This means any study of the incident might include forestry and agriculture on the one hand, because the meteor destroyed so much wood and farmland, and astronomy on the other, because it reached the Earth from space.

In research studies the facts you need are often related to people. Who unified Germany? Where did General Gordon die? What theory did Einstein put forward? When they're not related to people, they're generally related to each other. Question: what were the implications of silicon technology? Answer: we could afford personal computers.

All these things are, of course, linkages and if you've worked through the book this far, remembering linkages should be second nature to you by now. Let's see how the basic principles can be put to work to cram your head full of facts on just about any subject that might interest you, starting with facts related to people.

How to learn history

Let's suppose you're studying the life and hard times of Otto von Bismarck.

There are a lot of things you might want to link with Bismarck – the fact that he was sent as ambassador to Leningrad, the fact that he attended the Congress of Berlin, the Franco-German War of 1870-71, the fact that he unified Germany.

Your first step is to picture Bismarck. If you happen to know what he really looked like, you can use this as your starting point. Even if you only think you know what he looked like (because you saw a movie about him, for instance) you can still use this as your starting point.

But if you don't, you need to make a picture of his name. You do this in exactly the same way that you put pictures to the names in Chapter Ten. A fairly obvious approach might be to take the basic unit of German currency – the mark – and see it scuttling around busily in your mind's eye: a busy mark. But, as always, your ridiculous associations will work best for you.

Your next step is to make the link with the first fact you want to remember. Let's suppose it's the most important one – the unification of Germany. Picture that in some symbolic form and make the link. I'd visualize a fragmented map of Germany, then have the busy mark pushing the pieces together. You would obviously use your own picture.

With this done, you'd then continue to forge your daisy-chain of facts in the usual way.

Two-way street

The great thing about fact-links is that they work both ways.

What was Bismarck's major claim to fame? Bismarck becomes the busy mark which you immediately visualize as pushing Germany together. So Bismarck's major claim to fame was the unification of Germany.

Who unified Germany? Your mind pictures Germany in a fragmented state and at once into the mental picture races that busy mark to put it all together again. Busy Mark,

Bismarck, was the one who unified Germany.

You can use this system to link any sort of fact to any person, living or dead. Picture Adolf Hitler doing a goose-step up and down a pole to remind you it was the invasion of Poland that started the Second World War. Visualize Napoleon squashed by a Wellington boot to remind you who put paid to him at last. You will, of course, usually go on to daisy-chain a whole host of facts together.

What happens if your starting point has more than one meaning? *Bismarck* isn't just the Iron Chancellor – it's the capital of North Dakota, a German battleship in the Second World War, a range of mountains in New Guinea, a sea that forms part of the Pacific Ocean and an archipelago in that sea. Won't that confuse your daisy-chain?

In fact, context makes sure your chain remains intact. If somebody asks you who unified Germany, you don't start wondering if it was that battleship in the Second World War.

If linking people to facts is simple, linking facts to facts is easier still. Assume you need to remember something really obscure – like where a bird called the button quail builds her nest.

Your first step, exactly as before, is to visualize the button quail. It's a six-inch-long dull-coloured bird with short, rounded wings. But if you didn't know that, or were having trouble with the picture, you can make a ridiculous picture out of the name – a button that quails in the face of danger might do the trick.

Now move on to visualizing the habitat in the form of a ridiculous association. The habitat is the scrubby grasslands in the warmer regions of Europe – *warm scrub*. So you might visualize a trembling button sweating while it scrubs grass under a blazing sun.

The whole picture is perfectly ludicrous … and for that

very reason, it works. Another fact is tattooed onto your brain.

If you decide to link information blocks to keywords in this way, use your locus to link the keywords themselves, rather than daisy-chaining. That way there's less chance of getting lost in a maze of daisy-chains.

Using the Keyword System

This Keyword System can be used on almost any type of textbook article. When you become really familiar with it, you'll find you can actually select keywords and make links *as you go along*. Until that time comes, jot down the keywords in a notebook, then use your right brain techniques to remember them afterwards.

One interesting thing about the system is that you can apply it to material you create yourself. You know the problem. You prepare a project, then get so nervous you can't remember a thing when you have to present it.

The Keyword System is a fabulous insurance policy. Use it exactly the way you'd use it to remember a textbook article. Write your speech or project, then analyse its basic information pattern and list the relevant keywords.

Alternatively, you can build your speech or project round a series of keywords – many people do that anyway, since it forces you to organize your thoughts in advance.

Suppose, for example, you were preparing a piece on the Duke of Wellington. Your keywords might include:

Dublin ... *where he was born.* **India** ... *where he developed as a soldier.* **Salamanca** ... *where he trounced 40,000 French troops at*

166

the rate of 1,000 a minute. **Napoleon** *... his greatest enemy.* **Waterloo** *... where he beat Napoleon.* **Liverpool** *... because he joined the Earl of Liverpool's Tory Cabinet.* **Prime Minister** *... which was the post he reached in 1828.*

Having selected your keywords, you can then link any necessary information blocks – the Irish influence on the Duke's early life, Napoleon's mistake in dismissing him as a 'Sepoy General', how he became involved in the European wars, and so on.

When you've done this, stuff the whole lot into a visualization of a Wellington boot – the same one you just used to squash Napoleon. It may be an undignified way to think of one of Britain's greatest soldiers, but it will help you remember.

Chapter 17

MEMORY

The magic of music

Here's something you're not going to believe. Research shows rock music weakens you.

You can check out this mind-blowing piece of information for yourself. Have a friend stand with his or her right arm stretched out at shoulder height. Explain you're going to try to pull the arm down and you want them to resist with all their strength. Go ahead and try.

You may be able to pull the arm down or you may not – the actual result depends on the relative strength of your friend and yourself – but whether or not you succeed isn't the point. The point is for you to find out how easy or hard it is to move the arm.

Now, let your friend rest, then repeat the experiment. But this time, before you try to pull down the arm, put any rock music on the sound system and play it for about three minutes. Leave the room while the music is playing (so it won't affect you) but make sure your friend listens.

Come back, switch off the music, and try to pull down the arm. You'll find your friend is noticeably weaker. This isn't your imagination. Tests in London using machine measurements and Led Zeppelin have shown conclusively that listening to rock music weakens you.

It gets more weird. Experiments at the Annamalai University of India showed that recorded lute music played to balsam plants produced 20% better growth and a massive 70% more leaves when compared with control plants that were left silent. When music was played in the paddy fields, rice harvests jumped between 20 and 60%.

But everything depends on the type of music you play. A research programme in Denver had both classical and rock music played to flowers. When serenaded with Haydn, Brahms, Bach and Beethoven, they outgrew control plants and leaned towards the speakers. When exposed to rock, they leaned away from the speakers and died within two weeks.

Classical music seems to work on people too. French research suggests Mozart co-ordinates breathing, heart and brain wave rhythms and improves your health. If you play Mozart on your Walkman while cycling, it has a good influence on how well you judge space and distance, so you should hit fewer pedestrians, but can you hear that car sneaking up behind you?

Fascinating though this is, what's it got to do with memory?

Introducing: Memory Music

All your right brain visualizing is properly called auto-genics. For many years now, the most intensive scientific study of autogenics has been done in Eastern Europe and particularly the old Soviet Union, before it fell apart. One thing to come out of this study is that memory visualization works better if you do it to a certain type of music – something called baroque.

Baroque music goes back to the 18th Century. Maybe the most interesting story about it involves the great composer Johann Sebastian Bach. At one stage of his career, Bach was called on by the Russian Envoy, Count Kayserling, to help with his difficulty sleeping.

Kayserling had it in mind that a little light music might be of benefit. So he asked Bach to compose something bright and interesting, but calm. Only too happy to earn a fat fee, Bach went off and did so.

When Bach delivered the piece, Kayserling hired a musician called Goldberg to play it. The piece worked like a charm. Only minutes after the music began, Kayserling felt the tensions beginning to drain from his body. Soon he was fast asleep. Goldberg stopped playing and crept away to his own bed.

From then on, Kayserling slept a great deal better than Goldberg, who had to sit up with his harpsichord in case he was required to play Bach's special sleep music again. Each time he did so, Kayserling dozed off promptly. The music that did the trick is now known as the *Goldberg Variations*.

This may sound like a very long-winded way of saying music helps you relax, but it goes further than that. Unless you're over-tired to begin with, a particular type of music helps you memorize things better.

It's the beat that counts

The key to the effect is the tempo. If the music you're listening to plays at (or near) sixty beats a minute, it will do the trick. It doesn't have to be classical. It can be pop, new age, jazz, whatever, just so long as the beat is right. But keep away from anything with vocals, which will only distract you, and remember that stringed instruments seem to give the best results.

Once again, this is something you can easily test for yourself. Here's a list of suitable pieces arranged alphabetically by composer. You can mix and match them to put together your own selection to use as 'memory music' while you study.

Bach

Largo from the Concerto in G Minor for Flute and Strings
Aria to *The Goldberg Variations* (BWV 988)
Largo from the Harpsichord Concerto in F Minor (BWV 1056)
Adagio from the Solo Harpsichord Concerto in D Minor

(BWV 1052)
Siciliano from the Solo Harpsichord Concerto in E Major
(BWV 1053)
Andante from the Solo Harpsichord Concerto in F Major
(BWV 1057)

Corelli
Sarabanda from Concerto No. 7 in D Major
Prelude and sarabanda from the Concerto No. 8 in E Minor
Preludio from Concerto No. 9 in A Major
Sarabanda from Concerto No. 10 in F Major

Handel
From *Music for the Royal Fireworks*:
Largo from Concerto No. 1 in F op.
Largo from Concerto No. 3 in D minor op.
From Concerto No. 1 in B-flat Major:
Largo from Concerto No. 1 in B-flat Major op.

Telemann
Largo from Double Fantasia in G Major for Harpsichord
Largo from Concerto in G Major for Viola and String
Orchestra

Vivaldi
Largo from Winter, in *The Four Seasons*
Largo from Concerto in D Major for Guitar and Strings in
Baroque Guitar Concerti
Largo from Concerto in C Major for Mandolin, Strings and
Harpsichord
Largo from Concerto in D Minor for Viola D'Amore,
Strings and Harpsichord
Largo from Concerto in F Major for Viola D'Amore, Two
Oboes, Bassoon, Two Horns and Figured Brass

Largo from Flute Concerto No. 4 in G Major
Vivaldi 6 Flute Concerti, Op. 10

Your aim is to put together a programme which runs for the length of your visualization sessions, so you don't need all that much.

Do-It-Yourself

If you play an instrument yourself – especially a stringed instrument like a violin or guitar – there's nothing to stop you recording your own 'memory music'. Just make sure the tempo is at, or very close to, 60 beats a minute.

Which brings us to the heart of the matter. What works in memory music is the rhythm. Because rhythm results in something called entrainment. To understand entrainment, you need to know about two things. One of them is brain waves. The other is Voodoo drumming.

Voodoo, as you're probably aware, is the religion of Haiti, in the West Indies. It's a mixture of old African and native West Indian faiths along with some Roman Catholic liturgy and sacraments. A feature of the cult is that at special ceremonies the loa, or gods of Voodoo, occupy the bodies of their worshippers. Anybody possessed in this way behaves and acts as the loa directs, usually dancing wildly to the point of exhaustion.

For years experts thought this sort of thing happened because the Voodoo faithful believed it would happen. In other words they talked themselves into it. But then a European traveller attended a Voodoo ceremony. He didn't believe in the loa, but one of them got him just the same. He spent a happy, if confused, few hours dancing wildly with the best of them.

Quite clearly there was something more than blind faith at work. That something is connected with the way your brain works.

Your brain, apart from containing more cells than there are stars in the sky, also comes equipped with about 100,000,000,000 neurons which generate and pass along electrical signals. While each one is tiny, when you put them together they generate enough juice to be measured outside the brain. The machine that does this is called an electroencephalograph or EEG. The pattern produced on its read-out is known as a brain *wave*.

If you were looking at an EEG read-out, what you'd see would be an irregular, but repetitive wave-form. That's to say, the line is spiky all the way along, but it rises and falls in a predictable pattern.

All brain waves have a frequency which is measured in cycles per second, referred to as Hertz or Hz. If you read that something is, say, 10 Hz, it means the frequency is ten cycles per second.

If you're finding this heavy going, here's where it gets interesting. Some years ago, scientists discovered that your state of mind showed up in your brain wave patterns. What states of mind are we talking about? Five main patterns have been recognized.

First, there's your normal waking state, the one in which you spend most of your day. It's characterized by what are called Beta waves, running between 15 and 30 Hz.

Next, there's what's called the Alpha state, in which you generate waves at 7 to 14 Hz. When you go Alpha, you feel very relaxed, but awake. A lot of people start to generate Alpha when they meditate. Going into a hypnotic trance will do the trick as well.

Next, you have Theta waves, between 4 and 7 Hz. The best example of that state is when you're on the point of

175

falling asleep, but haven't actually done so. You're not quite awake, not quite asleep. Your mind is floating and the chances are you're getting dream-like glimpses of mental images and sounds. Deep trance can sometimes push you into this state.

When you finally fall asleep, you generate Delta waves between 0.5 and 4 Hz. This is deep sleep, without dreaming. Interestingly, when you dream, the brain delivers bursts of Beta up to 30 Hz, a rate normally associated with waking consciousness.

Finally, they've recently discovered a very alert state which is associated with what are called Super-Beta waves, generating 30-40 Hz. Get into that one and you're high: you notice everything and your thoughts are crystal clear.

These patterns arise naturally, depending on what you're doing. At the moment you're probably generating Beta. Last night, when you were asleep, you were generating Delta. But that's not really to say your state of mind *causes* a particular pattern. The two simply go together. So, while you can trigger a particular wave pattern by getting into the right state of mind, you can also trigger the right state of mind by switching on its particular brain wave.

The way you do that is entrainment. Entrainment is the word psychologists now use to describe something we've known about (without knowing we knew) all the way back to the Stone Age. This is the tendency of the human brain to synchronize its brain waves with any rhythm going on around it.

Here, in a nutshell, you have the secret of Voodoo. Any loa ceremony involves a lot of rhythmic drumming. Whether you believe in Voodoo or not, if you hang in long enough your brain is going to try to synchronize itself with the rhythm of the drums. When that happens in Voodoo, you fall into a trance and dance under the instruction of the loa.

Rave rhythms and pop trance

It's also one reason why raves and pop concerts got to be so popular. Most pop music has a heavy beat. If you listen long enough, it will start to entrain your brain waves. If it's a particularly fast beat, it will push you up into the Super-Beta range, giving you extra energy for dancing. Other rhythms will actually pull you into a trance. It happens to lots of people without them even knowing, and explains things like head-banging.

When it happens with 60-beat music, your mind becomes better at visualization. If you get the rhythm right, there's also a separate effect on memory. The University of North Texas tested this out in 1982 with three groups of students and a recording of Handel's *Water Music*.

All three groups were required to learn a list of new words. Group 1 just read the list and tried to remember it. Group 2 read the list to the sound of Handel and tried to remember it. Group 3 used visualization to help them remember, and had the *Water Music* playing in the background as they did so.

Despite the fact that in earlier tests all three groups showed much the same memory abilities, the two groups using music had far better results than the group that tried to memorize without it. You'll not be surprised to hear that Group 3, which used visualization as well, held onto the information best of all three groups when tested again a week later.

The influence of music on memory is something that's been known for a very long time. More than two thousand years ago, audiences in Athens were treated to a special festival in the Panathenes every four years.

During the festival, the entire *Iliad* was chanted entirely from memory to the rhythmic playing of a lyre. Not only did the rhythm help the professional presenter, but many members of the audience also discovered they could remember long passages of the classic afterwards – a fact remarked on in the histories of the time.

Using 'memory music' is simplicity itself. Put together a tape of the type of 'memory music' you really enjoy. Once again, it can be anything that turns you on, just so long as the tempo is around 60 beats per minute. Make sure there's enough on the tape to cover your full study period. Hit the play button, adjust the volume so it's playing pleasantly in the background, then get on with your studies. You don't have to listen or do anything else. The effect on your memory is automatic.

Chapter 18

MEMORY

A master plan for
mega memory

Let's review the information so far. In doing so, this chapter will become your master plan for mega memory – a quick reference guide you can use as a refresher time and time again. Read your way through it carefully – there's a small reward at the very end.

1. There are *two parts* to memory. The first involves filing away information by transferring it from your short-term memory to your long-term memory. The second is recalling the information later. Here's a helpful diagram:

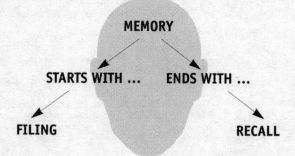

MEMORY

STARTS WITH ...   **ENDS WITH ...**

FILING   **RECALL**

2. Any effort you put into the right-hand side of that diagram is largely wasted. The place to put the effort is the left. In other words, you need to make your effort when you're *filing away* information, not when you're trying to recall it. This is the *exact opposite* of the way most people try to remember.

3. Memorizing the old way, by repeating something over and over, is boring, difficult and inefficient. The sooner you stop trying to memorize that way, the sooner you'll start to build a better memory.

4. Making pictures in your mind is the most important key to a mega memory. Anything filed visually is much, much easier to remember.

5. Emotional appeal gives your mental pictures added impact. Pictures that are dramatic, exciting, full of movement, exaggerated or rude are easiest of all to remember.

6. Mental 'pictures' which include smells, sounds, tastes and touch sensations have added impact, hence added memorability.

7. Since items that have *meaning* are far easier to remember than those that haven't, you should always try to *give meaning* to things you need to remember (by, for example, weaving them into a story). If you have to remember something that has no meaning in itself – like a long number – convert it into something else that does.

8. Attention, interest and observation all contribute to effective memory.

9. If you really can't remember something, peg it to something else you can.

There are three basic memory systems outlined in this book:

● **The Locus System**
    helps you memorize by creating a mental storehouse for items you want to remember. This can be a visualization of your own home or some other, larger building. (It's possible to work with a fictional locus, but one based on a real place works much better.) You can create a portable locus out of your own body.

● **The Link or Daisy-Chain System**
    helps you memorize by creating exaggerated, dramatic or ridiculous links between one item and another. This system follows the way your memory actually works, so that recalling one item will automatically bring up the associated links.

● **The Peg System**

helps you remember something difficult, like a number, by converting it into something easier and more meaningful to visualize. At a basic level, you can convert the ten digits 0 to 9 into pictures through rhyming associations or visual associations suggested by the shapes of the figures.

These three systems can be used together in any combination to help you remember different things. Pegs or daisy-chained items can be stored in a locus. Different loci can be daisy-chained together. The method given in this book for remembering names is a mixture of body locus, daisy-chain and peg systems.

While any or all of these three systems will dramatically improve your memory, you can do even better by using them alongside proven study techniques. The most powerful of these are:

1. Try studying to a soft, gentle background of 'memory (60 beats per minute) music'. This helps you relax and *automatically* improves your memory.
2. Find the *hidden patterns* in the material you're studying. When you discover how it's organized, remembering comes easier.
3. Learn how to extract *keywords* from the material you're studying. Then use your memory systems to remember the keywords.
4. Review your work every ten minutes, preferably by asking yourself questions about it.
5. Take a short break in study every half-hour if possible.
6. Hire a Voodoo drummer to play while you're reading. (Only kidding.)

7. Take a little exercise and get plenty of sleep, particularly early-morning dream sleep. The ideal is Early to Bed, but not Early to Rise. Get an early night and sleep in next morning. That way you're well rested and you get your maximum of dream sleep.

8. Take time to organize your material. The act of organizing *automatically* improves your recall.

When you see the whole thing put together like this, getting your memory into shape doesn't look too difficult. But there is one very serious problem.

Even though you'll find these techniques really work, even though none of them is difficult, even though they're more interesting and more fun than the old grindstone ways you were taught to remember, you'll *still* find you often neglect to put them into practice. Worse, you'll *still* find yourself trying to remember the bad, old way.

This may be daft, but it's also human nature. What you're experiencing is the force of habit. You were taught one way to remember, you've used it for years so even though you've found a better way, habit keeps you stuck.

The only one way to escape your old habit is to replace it with a new one. Which really means *forcing* yourself to use the new right-brain visual techniques for a while, until they become second nature to you. It'll be a hassle at first, but believe me it's well worth it.

How to impress the pants off everybody

But enough of motivation. Here's your reward for reading this far – a technique that's utterly useless except for one small thing: it will impress the pants off anybody.

This technique lets you instantly name the day that

matches any given date throughout the year.

How's it done?

You need a little preparation. Find a calendar and use it to discover the date of the *first Sunday* of each month throughout the year.

In 1996, for example, the first Sunday of January was on 7 January, the first Sunday of February was 4 February, the first Sunday of March was 3 March, the first Sunday of April was 7 April and so on.

If you look up the calendar for 1997, you'll find the first Sunday of January is 5 January, February is 2 February, March is 2 March, April is 6 April, May is 4 May and so on.

What you do next is write down the numbers of the first Sundays for your current year, giving you a twelve-digit number. As an example, the number for 1997 is:

522641637527

This number is all you need to 'remember' the date of every day throughout the year. You need to commit that number to memory. Do it using the peg method:

522641637527 becomes hive ... shoe ... shoe ... sticks ... door ... bun ... sticks ... tree ... heaven ... hive ... shoe ... heaven.

Now challenge a friend to give you a date. Let's suppose the date they give you is 19 July.

According to the number you've just memorized, the first

Sunday of July (in 1997) falls on 6 July. (July is the seventh month, so count seven digits of your number. By a miraculous coincidence, the date is the 6th. If you'd been asked for August, you'd have counted eight digits and found the date of the first Sunday in August was the 3rd.)

Once you have this information, you can calculate that the second Sunday falls on 13 July, the third on 20 July and the fourth on 27 July. At first you'll do this by adding seven for each succeeding week. Once you get the hang of it, you'll short-cut by multiplying.

Since 20 July is a Sunday, it follows that 19 July, the date you're looking for, has to be the day before – a Saturday.

Play around with this a few times with a calendar in your hand to check your answers. Once you've gained speed and confidence, you can put a day to any date in the year within seconds.

Chapter 19

Quick Memory Test
(To be taken **only** when
you've read this book)

MEMORY

Here's a quick way to find out how much your memory has improved since you read this book. Answer each question, then move on to the *How to score* section to work out how you did.

1. Without looking, write down the first four words of the first chapter of this book. (Not the Introduction, the first chapter.)

2. In Chapter Two, you worked on a list of 30 items beginning Deck of Cards, Quartz Crystal, Australian Aborigine etc. Without checking, see how many items on that list you can still remember.

3. Here's a brand new list you've never seen before. Memorize it using the peg method. You'll be asked a question about it when you come to check your score.

> 1. A dollar bill
> 2. A parrot
> 3. An island
> 4. A women's magazine
> 5. A soldier
> 6. A cargo ship
> 7. A palm tree
> 8. A scotsman's kilt
> 9. A parking meter
> 10. A windmill

4. Name this man.

5. Memorize this number any way you like: **01715283154**.

How to score

1. The first four words of the first chapter were 'You are absolutely incredible.' Score 5 points for every word you remembered.
2. Check the list now. If you remembered fewer than 10 items, score zero. If you remembered between 10 and 20 items, score 10. If you remembered more than 20 items, score 20.
3. Without looking, write down the eighth item on the list. If you got it right, score 20. If you got it wrong, but your answer figured somewhere on the list, score 5. Otherwise score zero.
4. It's your old friend Maurice Maeterlinck. If you knew that, score 20. If you didn't, score zero.
5. Without looking, write down the number you memorized. If you get it right, score 20. If you get one digit wrong (or misplaced) score 5. Otherwise, score zero.

How you rate

Score 100:	You should be on stage. Your memory's right up there with stars like Harry Lorayne. Are you sure you didn't peek?
80 – 95:	This is the high range of memory. What you've got places you in the top 10% of the population.
60 – 80:	You're way above average. Keep using the techniques and you'll keep improving.
40 – 60:	You're still above average, believe it or not, but that's only because most people have such lousy memories. Keep working at it – there's room for improvement.
under 40:	Read the book again – and concentrate this time!

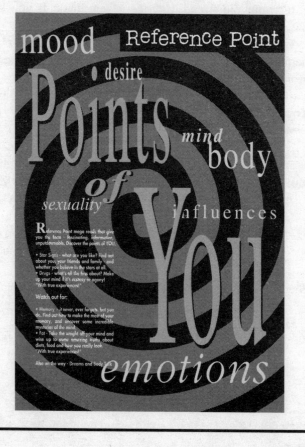